FOR:_____

FROM:_____

*A wise man's heart guides his mouth,
and his lips promote instruction.*

Proverbs 20:15

Daily Inspiration for Teachers from the New International Version
Copyright © 2005 by The Zondervan Corporation
ISBN-10: 0-310-81005-1
ISBN-13: 978-0-310-81005-6

Requests for information should be addressed to:
Inspirio, The gift group of Zondervan
Grand Rapids, Michigan 49530
http://www.inspiriogifts.com

Compiler: June Gunden
Project Manager: Tom Dean
Design Manager: Kathy Needham
Cover Design: Michael J. Williams
Interior Design: Anne Huizenga

Printed in the United States of America
05 06 07/OPM/ 4 3 2 1

Daily Inspiration
for TEACHERS

from the New International Version

inspirio™

Contents

Contents

Contents

Introduction

The teaching profession is both highly esteemed and not esteemed enough. As a teacher you have no doubt felt times of frustration, weakness, and even a temptation to quit or to do less than your best, because of the unique stresses of your job.

God's Word can help you! The Bible gives strength, encouragement, and guidance to all who seek. "God is faithful; he will not let you be tempted beyond what you can bear. But when you are tempted, he will also provide a way out so that you can stand up under it" (1 Corinthians 10:13).

What you are doing is so important to the life of every student whose life you touch. Our prayer is that God will, through these Scriptures, give you the strength you need to be an outstanding teacher.

Daily Inspiration for Teachers from the New International Version brings you an entire year of Bible readings, helping you to listen to God every day. Start at the beginning of the year on Week 1, or start in the middle of the year with a topic that interests you most. Any way you use it, Daily Inspiration for Teachers will give you help and encouragement all year long!

Week 1: Monday

If any of you lacks wisdom, he should ask God, who gives generously to all without finding fault, and it will be given to him. But when he asks, he must believe and not doubt, because he who doubts is like a wave of the sea, blown and tossed by the wind.

—*James 1:5–6*

*The fear of the LORD teaches a man wisdom,
    and humility comes before honor.*

—**Proverbs 15:33**

Where is the wise man? Where is the scholar? Where is the philosopher of this age? Has not God made foolish the wisdom of the world? For since in the wisdom of God the world through its wisdom did not know him, God was pleased through the foolishness of what was preached to save those who believe. Jews demand miraculous signs and Greeks look for wisdom, but we preach Christ crucified: a stumbling block to Jews and foolishness to Gentiles, but to those whom God has called, both Jews and Greeks, Christ the power of God and the wisdom of God. For the foolishness of God is wiser than man's wisdom, and the weakness of God is stronger than man's strength.

—**1 Corinthians 1:20–25**

Week 1: Tuesday

The holy Scriptures ... are able to make you wise for salvation through faith in Jesus Christ. All Scripture is God-breathed and is useful for teaching, rebuking, correcting and training in righteousness, so that the man of God may be thoroughly equipped for every good work.

—*2 Timothy 3:15–17*

The word of God is living and active. Sharper than any double-edged sword, it penetrates even to dividing soul and spirit, joints and marrow; it judges the thoughts and attitudes of the heart.

—*Hebrews 4:12*

Oh, how I love your law!
I meditate on it all day long.
Your commands make me wiser than my enemies,
for they are ever with me.
I have more insight than all my teachers,
for I meditate on your statutes.
I have more understanding than the elders,
for I obey your precepts.

—*Psalm 119:97–100*

Week 1: Wednesday

Where does wisdom come from?
Where does understanding dwell?
It is hidden from the eyes of every living thing,
concealed even from the birds of the air.
Destruction and Death say,
"Only a rumor of it has reached our ears."
God understands the way to it
and he alone knows where it dwells,
for he views the ends of the earth
and sees everything under the heavens.
When he established the force of the wind
and measured out the waters,
when he made a decree for the rain
and a path for the thunderstorm,
then he looked at wisdom and appraised it;
he confirmed it and tested it.
And he said to man,
"The fear of the Lord—that is wisdom,
and to shun evil is understanding."

—Job 28:20–28

Week 1: Thursday

Hold on to instruction, do not let it go;
guard it well, for it is your life.
Do not set foot on the path of the wicked
or walk in the way of evil men.
Avoid it, do not travel on it;
turn from it and go on your way.
For they cannot sleep till they do evil;
they are robbed of slumber till they make
someone fall.
They eat the bread of wickedness
and drink the wine of violence.

The path of the righteous is like the first gleam of
dawn,
shining ever brighter till the full light of day.
But the way of the wicked is like deep darkness;
they do not know what makes them stumble.

—Proverbs 4:13–19

Week 1: Friday

Do not deceive yourselves. If any one of you thinks he is wise by the standards of this age, he should become a "fool" so that he may become wise. For the wisdom of this world is foolishness in God's sight. As it is written: "He catches the wise in their craftiness"; and again, "The Lord knows that the thoughts of the wise are futile." So then, no more boasting about men! All things are yours, whether Paul or Apollos or Cephas or the world or life or death or the present or the future—all are yours, and you are of Christ, and Christ is of God.

—1 Corinthians 3:18–23

Wisdom says:
"Counsel and sound judgment are mine;
*   I have understanding and power.*
By me kings reign
*   and rulers make laws that are just;*
by me princes govern,
*   and all nobles who rule on earth.*
I love those who love me,
*   and those who seek me find me."*

—Proverbs 8:14–17

Week 1: Weekend

Listen and hear my voice;
*   pay attention and hear what I say.*
When a farmer plows for planting, does he plow
continually?
*   Does he keep on breaking up and harrowing*
*   the soil?*
When he has leveled the surface,
*   does he not sow caraway and scatter cummin?*
Does he not plant wheat in its place,
*   barley in its plot,*
*   and spelt in its field?*
His God instructs him
*   and teaches him the right way.*

Caraway is not threshed with a sledge,
*   nor is a cartwheel rolled over cummin;*
caraway is beaten out with a rod,
*   and cummin with a stick.*
Grain must be ground to make bread;
*   so one does not go on threshing it forever.*
Though he drives the wheels of his threshing cart
over it,
*   his horses do not grind it.*
All this also comes from the LORD Almighty,
*   wonderful in counsel and magnificent in wisdom.*

—Isaiah 28:23–29

Week 2: Monday

Tell the righteous it will be well with them,
for they will enjoy the fruit of their deeds.

—*Isaiah 3:10*

"For I know the plans I have for you," declares the LORD,
"plans to prosper you and not to harm you, plans to
give you hope and a future. Then you will call upon me
and come and pray to me, and I will listen to you."

—*Jeremiah 29:11–12*

Consider what God has done:

Who can straighten
what he has made crooked?
When times are good, be happy;
but when times are bad, consider:
God has made the one
as well as the other.
Therefore a man cannot discover
anything about his future.

—*Ecclesiastes 7:13–14*

Week 2: Tuesday

Wait for the LORD
and keep his way.
He will exalt you to inherit the land;
when the wicked are cut off, you will see it.

I have seen a wicked and ruthless man
flourishing like a green tree in its native soil,
but he soon passed away and was no more;
though I looked for him, he could not be found.

Consider the blameless, observe the upright;
there is a future for the man of peace.

—Psalm 37:34–37

Do not let your heart envy sinners,
but always be zealous for the fear of the LORD.
There is surely a future hope for you,
and your hope will not be cut off.

—Proverbs 23:17–18

Week 2: Wednesday

The LORD is good to those whose hope is in him, to the one who seeks him.

—Lamentations 3:25

I trust in you, O LORD;
*   I say, "You are my God."*
My times are in your hands.

—Psalm 31:14–15

Hope does not disappoint us, because God has poured out his love into our hearts by the Holy Spirit, whom he has given us.

—Romans 5:5

Week 2: Thursday

Where can I go from your Spirit?
Where can I flee from your presence?
If I go up to the heavens, you are there;
if I make my bed in the depths, you are there.
If I rise on the wings of the dawn,
if I settle on the far side of the sea,
even there your hand will guide me,
your right hand will hold me fast. ...

For you created my inmost being;
you knit me together in my mother's womb.
I praise you because I am fearfully and wonderfully
made;
your works are wonderful,
I know that full well.
My frame was not hidden from you
when I was made in the secret place.
When I was woven together in the depths of the earth,
your eyes saw my unformed body.

All the days ordained for me
were written in your book
before one of them came to be.

—Psalm 139:7–10, 13–16

Week 2: Friday

The fear of the LORD adds length to life.

—Proverbs 10:27

In the house of the wise are stores of choice food and oil,
*   but a foolish man devours all he has.*

—Proverbs 21:20

The race is not to the swift
*   or the battle to the strong,*
nor does food come to the wise
*   or wealth to the brilliant*
*   or favor to the learned;*
but time and chance happen to them all.

—Ecclesiastes 9:11

Do not boast about tomorrow
*   for you do not know what a day may bring forth.*

—Proverbs 27:1

Week 2: **Weekend**

*Trust in the LORD with all your heart
    and lean not on your own understanding;
in all your ways acknowledge him,
    and he will make your paths straight.*

—Proverbs 3:5–6

This is what the LORD says:

*"Restrain your voice from weeping
    and your eyes from tears,
for your work will be rewarded,"
    declares the LORD.
There is hope for your future,"
    declares the LORD.*

—Jeremiah 31:16–17

Week 3: Monday

Let us not become weary in doing good, for at the proper time we will reap a harvest if we do not give up. Therefore, as we have opportunity, let us do good to all people, especially to those who belong to the family of believers.

—Galatians 6:9–10

Blessed is the man who perseveres under trial, because when he has stood the test, he will receive the crown of life that God has promised to those who love him.

—James 1:12

*Let us acknowledge the LORD;
    let us press on to acknowledge him.
As surely as the sun rises,
    he will appear;
he will come to us like the winter rains,
    like the spring rains that water the earth.*

—Hosea 6:3

Week 3: Tuesday

Let us throw off everything that hinders and the sin that so easily entangles, and let us run with perseverance the race marked out for us.

—Hebrews 12:1

Jesus . . . told this parable:
"A farmer went out to sow his seed. As he was scattering the seed, some fell . . . on good soil. It came up and yielded a crop, a hundred times more than was sown.

"The seed on good soil stands for those with a noble and good heart, who hear the word, retain it, and by persevering produce a crop."

—Luke 8:4–5, 8, 15

For God, who said, "Let light shine out of darkness," made his light shine in our hearts to give us the light of knowledge of the glory of God in the face of Christ. We have this treasure in jars of clay to show that this all-surpassing power is from God and not from us. We are hard pressed on every side, but not crushed; perplexed, but not in despair; persecuted, but not abandoned; struck down, but not destroyed.

—2 Corinthians 4:6–9

Week 3: Wednesday

Consider it pure joy, my brothers, whenever you face trials of many kinds, because you know that the testing of your faith develops perseverance. Perseverance must finish its work so that you may be mature and complete, not lacking anything.

—**James 1:2–4**

I will exalt you, O LORD,
for you lifted me out of the depths
and did not let my enemies gloat over me.
O LORD my God, I called to you for help
and you healed me.
O LORD, you brought me up from the grave;
you spared me from going down into the pit.

Sing to the LORD, you saints of his;
praise his holy name.
For his anger lasts only a moment,
but his favor lasts a lifetime;
weeping may remain for a night,
but rejoicing comes in the morning.

—**Psalm 30:1–5**

Week 3: Thursday

Turn to me and be gracious to me,
for I am lonely and afflicted.
The troubles of my heart have multiplied;
free me from my anguish.
Look upon my affliction and my distress
and take away all my sins.
See how my enemies have increased
and how fiercely they hate me!
Guard my life and rescue me;
let me not be put to shame,
for I take refuge in you.
May integrity and uprightness protect me,
because my hope is in you, O LORD.

—Psalm 25:16–21

We . . . rejoice in our sufferings, because we know that suffering produces perseverance; perseverance, character; and character, hope. And hope does not disappoint us, because God has poured out his love into our hearts by the Holy Spirit, whom he has given us.

—Romans 5:3–5

Week 3: Friday

Do not throw away your confidence; it will be richly rewarded. You need to persevere so that when you have done the will of God, you will receive what he has promised. For in just a very little while,

"He who is coming will come and will not delay.
    But my righteous one will live by faith.
And if he shrinks back,
    I will not be pleased with him."

But we are not of those who shrink back and are destroyed,
but of those who believe and are saved.

—Hebrews 10:35–39

I have fought the good fight, I have finished the race, I have kept the faith.

—2 Timothy 4:7

Week 3: Weekend

Jesus said, "I know your deeds, your hard work and your perseverance. I know that you cannot tolerate wicked men, that you have tested those who claim to be apostles but are not, and have found them false. You have persevered and have endured hardships for my name, and have not grown weary."

—Revelation 2:2–3

We pray . . . that you may live a life worthy of the Lord and may please him in every way: bearing fruit in every good work, growing in the knowledge of God, being strengthened with all power according to his glorious might so that you may have great endurance and patience, and joyfully giving thanks to the Father, who has qualified you to share in the inheritance of the saints in the kingdom of light.

—Colossians 1:10–12

Week 4: Monday

Jesus said,
"If you obey my commands, you will remain in my love,
just as I have obeyed my Father's commands and
remain in his love. I have told you this so that my joy
may be in you and that your joy may be complete."

—John 15:10–11

I will extol the LORD at all times;
*   his praise will always be on my lips.*
My soul will boast in the LORD;
*   let the afflicted hear and rejoice.*
Glorify the LORD with me;
*   let us exalt his name together.*

I sought the LORD, and he answered me;
*   he delivered me from all my fears.*
Those who look to him are radiant;
*   their faces are never covered with shame.*

—Psalm 34:1–5

Week 4: Tuesday

Be joyful always; pray continually; give thanks in all circumstances, for this is God's will for you in Christ Jesus.

—1 Thessalonians 5:16–18

Let the peace of Christ rule in your hearts, since as members of one body you were called to peace. And be thankful. Let the word of Christ dwell in you richly as you teach and admonish one another with all wisdom, and as you sing psalms, hymns and spiritual songs with gratitude in your hearts to God. And whatever you do, whether in word or deed, do it all in the name of the Lord Jesus, giving thanks to God the Father through him.

—Colossians 3:15–17

Rejoice in the Lord always. I will say it again: Rejoice!

—Philippians 4:4

A fool finds pleasure in evil conduct,
*   but a man of understanding delights in wisdom.*

—Proverbs 10:23

Week 4: Wednesday

An anxious heart weighs a man down,
but a kind word cheers him up.

—Proverbs 12:25

A happy heart makes the face cheerful.

—Proverbs 15:13

The cheerful heart has a continual feast.

—Proverbs 15:15

God will yet fill your mouth with laughter
and your lips with shouts of joy.

—Job 8:21

*This is the day the L*ord *has made;*
let us rejoice and be glad in it.

—Psalm 118:24

Week 4: Thursday

The joy of the LORD is your strength.

> —*Nehemiah 8:10*

Hear, O LORD, and be merciful to me;
*   O LORD, be my help."*

You turned my wailing into dancing;
*   you removed my sackcloth and clothed me*
*   with joy,*
that my heart may sing to you and not be silent.
*   O LORD my God, I will give you thanks forever.*

> —*Psalm 30:10–12*

When God gives any man wealth and possessions, and enables him to enjoy them, to accept his lot and be happy in his work—this is a gift of God.

> —*Ecclesiastes 5:19*

Week 4: Friday

Be patient, then, brothers, until the Lord's coming. See how the farmer waits for the land to yield its valuable crop and how patient he is for the autumn and spring rains. You too, be patient and stand firm, because the Lord's coming is near.

—James 5:7–8

You have made known to me the path of life;
    you will fill me with joy in your presence, O LORD,
    with eternal pleasures at your right hand.

—Psalm 16:11

Give thanks to the LORD, call on his name;
    make known among the nations what he has done.
Sing to him, sing praise to him;
    tell of all his wonderful acts.
Glory in his holy name;
    let the hearts of those who seek the LORD rejoice.

—1 Chronicles 16:8–10

Week 4: Weekend

So then, just as you received Christ Jesus as Lord,
continue to live in him, rooted and built up in him,
strengthened in the faith as you were taught, and
overflowing with thankfulness.

—Colossians 2:6–7

I will rejoice in the LORD,
I will be joyful in God my Savior.

he Sovereign LORD is my strength;
he makes my feet like the feet of a deer,
he enables me to go on the heights.

—Habakkuk 3:18–19

Let all who take refuge in you be glad, O LORD;
let them ever sing for joy.
Spread your protection over them,
that those who love your name may rejoice in you.

—Psalm 5:11

Week 5: Monday

Zacchaeus stood up and said to the Lord, "Look, Lord! Here and now I give half of my possessions to the poor, and if I have cheated anybody out of anything, I will pay back four times the amount."

Jesus said to him, "Today salvation has come to this house, because this man, too, is a son of Abraham. For the Son of Man came to seek and to save what was lost."

—*Luke 19:8–10*

Samuel said to all Israel, "I have listened to everything you said to me and have set a king over you. Now you have a king as your leader. As for me, I am old and gray, and my sons are here with you. I have been your leader from my youth until this day. Here I stand. Testify against me in the presence of the LORD and his anointed. Whose ox have I taken? Whose donkey have I taken? Whom have I cheated? Whom have I oppressed? From whose hand have I accepted a bribe to make me shut my eyes? If I have done any of these, I will make it right."

—*1 Samuel 12:1–3*

Week 5: Tuesday

Jesus said, "Whoever can be trusted with very little can also be trusted with much, and whoever is dishonest with very little will also be dishonest with much. So if you have not been trustworthy in handling worldly wealth, who will trust you with true riches? And if you have not been trustworthy with someone else's property, who will give you property of your own?

"No servant can serve two masters. Either he will hate the one and love the other, or he will be devoted to the one and despise the other. You cannot serve both God and Money."

—Luke 16:10–13

Follow justice and justice alone, so that you may live and possess the land the LORD your God is giving you.

—Deuteronomy 16:20

Week 5: Wednesday

Honest scales and balances are from the LORD;
all the weights in the bag are of his making.

—Proverbs 16:11

Do not have two differing weights in your bag—one heavy, one light. Do not have two differing measures in your house—one large, one small. You must have accurate and honest weights and measures, so that you may live long in the land the LORD your God is giving you. For the LORD your God detests anyone who does these things, anyone who deals dishonestly.

—Deuteronomy 25:13–16

The integrity of the upright guides them,
but the unfaithful are destroyed by their duplicity.

—Proverbs 11:3

Week 5: Thursday

See to it, brothers, that none of you has a sinful, unbelieving heart that turns away from the living God. But
encourage one another daily, as long as it is called
Today, so that none of you may be hardened by sin's
deceitfulness.

—Hebrews 3:12–13

"Two things I ask of you, O LORD;
do not refuse me before I die:
Keep falsehood and lies far from me;
give me neither poverty nor riches,
but give me only my daily bread.
Otherwise, I may have too much and disown you
and say, 'Who is the LORD?'
Or I may become poor and steal,
and so dishonor the name of my God."

—Proverbs 30:7–9

Week 5: Friday

Do not trust in extortion
or take pride in stolen goods;
though your riches increase,
do not set your heart on them.

—Psalm 62:10

This is what the LORD says:

"Maintain justice
and do what is right,
for my salvation is close at hand
and my righteousness will soon be revealed."

—Isaiah 56:1

The LORD abhors dishonest scales,
but accurate weights are his delight.

—Proverbs 11:1

Week 5: Weekend

The man of integrity walks securely, but he who takes crooked paths will be found out.

—Proverbs 10:9

In everything set them an example by doing what is good. In your teaching show integrity, seriousness and soundness of speech that cannot be condemned, so that those who oppose you may be ashamed because they have nothing bad to say about us.

—Titus 2:7–8

Week 6: Monday

Live in harmony with one another; be sympathetic, love as brothers, be compassionate and humble. Do not repay evil with evil or insult with insult, but with blessing, because to this you were called so that you may inherit a blessing. For,

"Whoever would love life
*   and see good days*
must keep his tongue from evil
*   and his lips from deceitful speech.*
He must turn from evil and do good;
*   he must seek peace and pursue it.*
For the eyes of the Lord are on the righteous
*   and his ears are attentive to their prayer,*
but the face of the Lord is against those who do evil."

Who is going to harm you if you are eager to do good? But even if you should suffer for what is right, you are blessed.

—1 Peter 3:8–14

Week 6: Tuesday

Your attitude should be the same as that of Christ
Jesus:

Who, being in very nature God,
 did not consider equality with God something to
 be grasped,
but made himself nothing,
 taking the very nature of a servant,
 being made in human likeness.
And being found in appearance as a man,
 he humbled himself
 and became obedient to death—
  even death on a cross!
Therefore God exalted him to the highest place
 and gave him the name that is above every name,
that at the name of Jesus every knee should bow,
 in heaven and on earth and under the earth,
and every tongue confess that Jesus Christ is Lord,
 to the glory of God the Father.

—Philippians 2:5–11

Week 6: Wednesday

It is by grace you have been saved, through faith—and this not from yourselves, it is the gift of God—not by works, so that no one can boast. For we are God's workmanship, created in Christ Jesus to do good works, which God prepared in advance for us to do.

—Ephesians 2:8–10

I kneel before the Father, from whom his whole family in heaven and on earth derives its name. I pray that out of his glorious riches he may strengthen you with power through his Spirit in your inner being, so that Christ may dwell in your hearts through faith. And I pray that you, being rooted and established in love, may have power, together with all the saints, to grasp how wide and long and high and deep is the love of Christ, and to know this love that surpasses knowledge—that you may be filled to the measure of all the fullness of God.

Now to him who is able to do immeasurably more than all we ask or imagine, according to his power that is at work within us, to him be glory in the church and in Christ Jesus throughout all generations, for ever and ever! Amen.

—Ephesians 3:14–21

Week 6: Thursday

Ever since I heard about your faith in the Lord Jesus and your love for all the saints, I have not stopped giving thanks for you, remembering you in my prayers. I keep asking that the God of our Lord Jesus Christ, the glorious Father, may give you the Spirit of wisdom and revelation, so that you may know him better. I pray also that the eyes of your heart may be enlightened in order that you may know the hope to which he has called you, the riches of his glorious inheritance in the saints, and his incomparably great power for us who believe. That power is like the working of his mighty strength, which he exerted in Christ when he raised him from the dead and seated him at his right hand in the heavenly realms, far above all rule and authority, power and dominion, and every title that can be given, not only in the present age but also in the one to come. And God placed all things under his feet and appointed him to be head over everything for the church, which is his body, the fullness of him who fills everything in every way.

—Ephesians 1:15–23

Week 6: Friday

We know that we have come to know him if we obey his commands. The man who says, "I know him," but does not do what he commands is a liar, and the truth is not in him. But if anyone obeys his word, God's love is truly made complete in him. This is how we know we are in him: Whoever claims to live in him must walk as Jesus did.

—1 John 2:3–6

Make every effort to live in peace with all men and to be holy; without holiness no one will see the Lord. See to it that no one misses the grace of God and that no bitter root grows up to cause trouble.

—Hebrews 12:14–15

The mind of sinful man is death, but the mind controlled by the Spirit is life and peace; the sinful mind is hostile to God. It does not submit to God's law, nor can it do so. Those controlled by the sinful nature cannot please God. You, however, are controlled not by the sinful nature but by the Spirit, if the Spirit of God lives in you.

—Romans 8:6–9

Week 6: Weekend

I consider that our present sufferings are not worth comparing with the glory that will be revealed in us. . . . The Spirit helps us in our weakness. We do not know what we ought to pray for, but the Spirit himself intercedes for us with groans that words cannot express. And he who searches our hearts knows the mind of the Spirit, because the Spirit intercedes for the saints in accordance with God's will.

—Romans 8:18, 26–27

So I say, live by the Spirit, and you will not gratify the desires of the sinful nature. For the sinful nature desires what is
contrary to the Spirit, and the Spirit what is contrary to the sinful nature. They are in conflict with each other, so that you do not do what you want. But if you are led by the Spirit, you are not under law.

—Galatians 5:16–18

Week 7: Monday

My soul finds rest in God alone;
my salvation comes from him.
He alone is my rock and my salvation;
he is my fortress, I will never be shaken. . . .

Find rest, O my soul, in God alone;
my hope comes from him.
He alone is my rock and my salvation;
he is my fortress, I will not be shaken.
My salvation and my honor depend on God;
he is my mighty rock, my refuge.
Trust in him at all times, O people;
pour out your hearts to him,
for God is our refuge.

—Psalm 62:1-2; 5-8

Week 7: Tuesday

Praise be to the Lord, to God our Savior,
who daily bears our burdens.

—Psalm 68:19

"I will refresh the weary and satisfy the faint," says the Lord.

—Jeremiah 31:25

This is what the Sovereign LORD, the Holy One of Israel, says:

In repentance and rest is your salvation,
in quietness and trust is your strength."

—Isaiah 30:15

Of making many books there is no end, and much study wearies the body.

—Ecclesiastes 12:12

Week 7: **Wednesday**

*In vain you rise early
    and stay up late,
toiling for food to eat—
    for God grants sleep to those he loves.*

—Psalm 127:2

*Do not wear yourself out to get rich;
    have the wisdom to show restraint.*

—Proverbs 23:4

Jesus said,
"Come to me, all you who are weary and burdened, and
I will give you rest. Take my yoke upon you and learn
from me, for I am gentle and humble in heart, and you
will find rest for your souls. For my yoke is easy and my
burden is light."

—Matthew 11:28–30

*I love the LORD, for he heard my voice;
    he heard my cry for mercy.
Because he turned his ear to me,
    I will call on him as long as I live ...*

*Be at rest once more, O my soul,
    for the LORD has been good to you.*

—Psalm 116:1–2, 7

Week 7: Thursday

Because so many people were coming and going that they did not even have a chance to eat, Jesus said to his disciples, "Come with me by yourselves to a quiet place and get some rest."
So they went away by themselves in a boat to a solitary place.

—Mark 6:31–32

The fruit of righteousness will be peace;
*   the effect of righteousness will be*
*   quietness and confidence forever.*

—Isaiah 32:17

"My Presence will go with you, and I will give you rest," says the LORD.

—Exodus 33:14

I will lie down and sleep in peace,
*   for you alone, O LORD,*
*   make me dwell in safety.*

—Psalm 4:8

Week 7: Friday

Do you not know?
    Have you not heard?
The LORD is the everlasting God,
    the Creator of the ends of the earth.
He will not grow tired or weary,
    and his understanding no one can fathom.
He gives strength to the weary
    and increases the power of the weak.

—*Isaiah 40:28–29*

Be strong in the Lord and in his mighty power.

—*Ephesians 6:10*

My heart is not proud, O LORD,
    my eyes are not haughty;
I do not concern myself with great matters
    or things too wonderful for me.
But I have stilled and quieted my soul;
    like a weaned child with its mother,
    like a weaned child is my soul within me.

O Israel, put your hope in the LORD
    both now and forevermore.

—*Psalm 131:1–3*

Week 7: **Weekend**

When you went out before your people, O God,
  when you marched through the wasteland,
the earth shook,
  the heavens poured down rain,
before God, the One of Sinai,
  before God, the God of Israel.
You gave abundant showers, O God;
  you refreshed your weary inheritance.
Your people settled in it,
  and from your bounty, O God, you provided for the poor.

—Psalm 68:7–10

The news about Jesus spread ... so that crowds of people came to hear him and to be healed of their sicknesses. But Jesus often withdrew to lonely places and prayed.

—Luke 5:15–16

Week 8: Monday

A perverse man stirs up dissension,
and a gossip separates close friends.

—Proverbs 16:28

The good man brings good things out of the good stored up in his heart, and the evil man brings evil things out of the evil stored up in his heart. For out of the overflow of his heart his mouth speaks.

—Luke 6:45

Let your conversation be always full of grace, seasoned with salt, so that you may know how to answer everyone.

—Colossians 4:6

A gossip betrays a confidence;
so avoid a man who talks too much.

—Proverbs 20:19

Week 8: Tuesday

He who conceals his hatred has lying lips,
and whoever spreads slander is a fool.

—Proverbs 10:18

Without wood a fire goes out;
without gossip a quarrel dies down.

—Proverbs 26:20

He who covers over an offense promotes love,
but whoever repeats the matter separates
close friends.

—Proverbs 17:9

Do not let any unwholesome talk come out of your mouths, but only what is helpful for building others up according to their needs, that it may benefit those who listen.

—Ephesians 4:29

Week 8: Wednesday

Paul writes to his friends:
I am afraid that when I come I may not find you as I want you to be . . . I fear that there may be quarreling, jealousy, outbursts of anger, factions, slander, gossip, arrogance and disorder.

—2 Corinthians 12:20

With his mouth the godless destroys his neighbor,
*   but through knowledge the righteous escape.*

—Proverbs 11:9

The mouth of the righteous man utters wisdom,
*   and his tongue speaks what is just.*
The law of his God is in his heart;
*   his feet do not slip.*

—Psalm 37:30–31

Week 8: Thursday

Do not go about spreading slander among your people.
Do not do anything that endangers your neighbor's life.
I am the LORD.

—Leviticus 19:16

The words of a gossip are like choice morsels;
*   they go down to a man's inmost parts.*

—Proverbs 18:8

Reckless words pierce like a sword,
*   but the tongue of the wise brings healing.*

—Proverbs 12:18

He who guards his mouth and his tongue
*   keeps himself from calamity.*

—Proverbs 21:23

Avoid godless chatter, because those who indulge in it
will become more and more ungodly.

—2 Timothy 2:16

Week 8: Friday

LORD, who may dwell in your sanctuary?
Who may live on your holy hill?

He whose walk is blameless
and who does what is righteous,
who speaks the truth from his heart
and has no slander on his tongue,
who does his neighbor no wrong
and casts no slur on his fellowman,
who despises a vile man
but honors those who fear the LORD,
who keeps his oath
even when it hurts,
who lends his money without usury
and does not accept a bribe against the innocent.

He who does these things
will never be shaken.

—Psalm 15:1–5

Week 8: Weekend

*A gossip betrays a confidence,
    but a trustworthy man keeps a secret.*

—Proverbs 11:13

*A man who lacks judgment derides his neighbor,
    but a man of understanding holds his tongue.*

—Proverbs 11:12

*If you argue your case with a neighbor,
    do not betray another man's confidence,
or he who hears it may shame you
    and you will never lose your bad reputation.*

—Proverbs 25:9–10

*A prudent man keeps his knowledge to himself,
    but the heart of fools blurts out folly.*

—Proverbs 12:23

Week 9: Monday

*I will instruct you and teach you in the way you should
go;*
*   I will counsel you and watch over you.*
Do not be like the horse or the mule,
*   which have no understanding*
but must be controlled by bit and bridle
*   or they will not come to you.*
Many are the woes of the wicked,
*   but the LORD's unfailing love*
*   surrounds the man who trusts in him.*

—Psalm 32:8–10

Many are the plans in a man's heart,
*   but it is the LORD's purpose that prevails.*

—Proverbs 19:21

O our God, . . . we have no power to face this vast army
that is attacking us. We do not know what to do, but
our eyes are
upon you.

—2 Chronicles 20:12

Week 9: Tuesday

God knows the way that I take;
when he has tested me, I will come forth as gold.
My feet have closely followed his steps;
I have kept to his way without turning aside.
I have not departed from the commands of his lips;
I have treasured the words of his mouth more than
my daily bread.

—Job 23:10–12

A man's steps are directed by the LORD.
How then can anyone understand his own way?

—Proverbs 20:24

Jesus said,
"Surely I am with you always, to the very end of
the age."

—Matthew 28:20

Teach me your way, O LORD,
and I will walk in your truth;
give me an undivided heart,
that I may fear your name.

—Psalm 86:11

Week 9: Wednesday

I know, O LORD, that a man's life is not his own;
*   it is not for man to direct his steps.*

—Jeremiah 10:23

As for God, his way is perfect;
*   the word of the LORD is flawless.*
He is a shield
*   for all who take refuge in him.*
For who is God besides the LORD?
*   And who is the Rock except our God?*
It is God who arms me with strength
*   and makes my way perfect.*
He makes my feet like the feet of a deer;
*   he enables me to stand on the heights.*
He trains my hands for battle;
*   my arms can bend a bow of bronze.*
You give me your shield of victory,
*   and your right hand sustains me;*
*   you stoop down to make me great.*
You broaden the path beneath me,
*   so that my ankles do not turn.*

—Psalm 18:30–36

Week 9: Thursday

Be careful to do what the LORD your God has commanded you; do not turn aside to the right or to the left. Walk in all the way that the LORD your God has commanded you, so that you may live and prosper and prolong your days in the land that you will possess.

—**Deuteronomy 5:32–33**

This is what the LORD says—
    your Redeemer, the Holy One of Israel:
"I am the LORD your God,
    who teaches you what is best for you,
    who directs you in the way you should go.
If only you had paid attention to my commands,
    your peace would have been like a river,
    your righteousness like the waves of the sea.
Your descendants would have been like the sand,
    your children like its numberless grains;
their name would never be cut off
    nor destroyed from before me."

—**Isaiah 48:17–19**

Week 9: Friday

Keep me safe, O God,
*   for in you I take refuge.*

I said to the L<small>ORD</small>, "You are my Lord;
*   apart from you I have no good thing."*
As for the saints who are in the land,
*   they are the glorious ones in whom is all my*
delight.
The sorrows of those will increase
*   who run after other gods.*
I will not pour out their libations of blood
*   or take up their names on my lips.*

L<small>ORD</small>, you have assigned me my portion and my cup;
*   you have made my lot secure.*
The boundary lines have fallen for me in pleasant
places;
*   surely I have a delightful inheritance.*

I will praise the L<small>ORD</small>, who counsels me;
*   even at night my heart instructs me.*
I have set the L<small>ORD</small> always before me.
Because he is at my right hand,
*   I will not be shaken.*

—Psalm 16:1–8

Week 9: Weekend

O people of Zion, who live in Jerusalem, you will weep
no more. How gracious he will be when you cry for
help! As soon as he hears, he will answer you.
Although the Lord gives you the bread of adversity and
the water of affliction, your teachers will be hidden no
more; with your own eyes you will see them. Whether
you turn to the right or to the left, your ears will hear a
voice behind you, saying, "This is the way; walk in it."

—*Isaiah 30:19–21*

He has showed you, O man, what is good.
*   And what does the LORD require of you?*
To act justly and to love mercy
*   and to walk humbly with your God.*

—*Micah 6:8*

Your word is a lamp to my feet
*   and a light for my path, O LORD.*

—*Psalm 119:105*

In his heart a man plans his course,
*   but the LORD determines his steps.*

—*Proverbs 16:9*

Week 10: Monday

We know that anyone born of God does not continue to sin; the one who was born of God keeps him safe, and the evil one cannot harm him. We know that we are children of God, and that the whole world is under the control of the evil one. We know also that the Son of God has come and has given us understanding, so that we may know him who is true. And we are in him who is true—even in his Son Jesus Christ. He is the true God and eternal life.

—1 John 5:18–20

Live in harmony with one another; be sympathetic, love as brothers, be compassionate and humble.

—I Peter 3:8

Week 10: Tuesday

Do not love the world or anything in the world. If anyone loves the world, the love of the Father is not in him. For everything in the world—the cravings of sinful man, the lust of his eyes and the boasting of what he has and does—comes not from the Father but from the world. The world and its desires pass away, but the man who does the will of God lives forever.

—1 John 2:15–17

Seek the LORD while he may be found;
*   call on him while he is near.*
Let the wicked forsake his way
*   and the evil man his thoughts.*
Let him turn to the LORD, and he will have mercy
*   on him,*
*   and to our God, for he will freely pardon.*

—Isaiah 55:6–7

Blessed are the pure in heart,
*   for they will see God.*

—Matthew 5:8

Week 10: Wednesday

Dear children, do not let anyone lead you astray. He who does what is right is righteous, just as he is righteous. He who does what is sinful is of the devil, because the devil has been sinning from the beginning. The reason the Son of God appeared was to destroy the devil's work. No one who is born of God will continue to sin, because God's seed remains in him; he cannot go on sinning, because he has been born of God. This is how we know who the children of God are and who the children of the devil are: Anyone who does not do what is right is not a child of God; nor is anyone who does not love his brother.

—*1 John 3:7–10*

The king of Egypt said to the Hebrew midwives, whose names were Shiphrah and Puah, "When you help the Hebrew women in childbirth and observe them on the delivery stool, if it is a boy, kill him; but if it is a girl, let her live." The midwives, however, feared God and did not do what the king of Egypt had told them to do; they let the boys live. . . . So God was kind to the midwives and the people increased and became even more numerous. And because the midwives feared God, he gave them families of their own.

—*Exodus 1:15–17, 20–21*

Week 10: Thursday

Flee the evil desires of youth, and pursue righteousness, faith, love and peace, along with those who call
on the Lord out of a pure heart. Don't have anything to
do with foolish and stupid arguments, because you
know they produce quarrels. And the Lord's servant
must not quarrel; instead, he must be kind to everyone,
able to teach, not resentful. Those who oppose him he
must gently instruct, in the hope that God will grant
them repentance leading them to a knowledge of the
truth, and that they will come to their senses and
escape from the trap of the devil, who has taken them
captive to do his will.

—2 Timothy 2:22–26

But mark this: There will be terrible times in the last
days. People will be lovers of themselves, lovers of
money, boastful, proud, abusive, disobedient to their
parents, ungrateful, unholy, without love, unforgiving,
slanderous, without self-control, brutal, not lovers of
the good, treacherous, rash, conceited, lovers of
pleasure rather than lovers of God—having a form of
godliness but denying its power. Have nothing to do
with them.

—2 Timothy 3:1–5

Week 10: Friday

When Joseph's master saw that the LORD was with him and that the LORD gave him success in everything he did, Joseph found favor in his eyes and became his attendant. Potiphar put him in charge of his household, and he entrusted to his care everything he owned. From the time he put him in charge of his household and of all that he owned, the LORD blessed the household of the Egyptian because of Joseph. The blessing of the LORD was on everything Potiphar had, both in the house and in the field. So he left in Joseph's care everything he had; with Joseph in charge, he did not concern himself with anything except the food he ate. Now Joseph was well-built and handsome, and after a while his master's wife took notice of Joseph and said, "Come to bed with me!" But he refused. "With me in charge," he told her, "my master does not concern himself with anything in the house; everything he owns he has entrusted to my care. No one is greater in this house than I am. My master has withheld nothing from me except you, because you are his wife. How then could I do such a wicked thing and sin against God?" And though she spoke to Joseph day after day, he refused to go to bed with her or even be with her.

—Genesis 39:3–10

Week 10: Weekend

The Lord showed me two baskets of figs placed in front of the temple of the Lord. One basket had very good figs, like those that ripen early; the other basket had very poor figs, so bad they could not be eaten.
Then the Lord asked me, "What do you see, Jeremiah?"
"Figs," I answered. "The good ones are very good, but the poor ones are so bad they cannot be eaten."
Then the word of the Lord came to me: "This is what the Lord, the God of Israel, says: 'Like these good figs, I regard as good the exiles from Judah, whom I sent away from this place to the land of the Babylonians. My eyes will watch over them for their good, and I will bring them back to this land. I will build them up and not tear them down; I will plant them and not uproot them. I will give them a heart to know me, that I am the Lord. They will be my people, and I will be their God, for they will return to me with all their heart.' "

—*Jeremiah 24:1–7*

Jesus said,
"If you belonged to the world, it would love you as its own. As it is, you do not belong to the world, but I have chosen you out of the world."

—*John 15:19*

Week 11: Monday

The proverbs of Solomon son of David, king of Israel:

for attaining wisdom and discipline;
for understanding words of insight;
for acquiring a disciplined and prudent life,
doing what is right and just and fair;
for giving prudence to the simple,
knowledge and discretion to the young—
et the wise listen and add to their learning,
and let the discerning get guidance—
for understanding proverbs and parables,
the sayings and riddles of the wise.

—Proverbs 1:1–6

Jesus said,
"Those whom I love I rebuke and discipline. So be earnest, and repent. Here I am! I stand at the door and knock. If anyone hears my voice and opens the door, I will come in and eat with him, and he with me. To him who overcomes, I will give the right to sit with me on my throne, just as I overcame and sat down with my Father on his throne."

—Revelation 3:19–21

Week II: Tuesday

*My son, do not despise the LORD's discipline
and do not resent his rebuke,
the LORD disciplines those he loves,
as a father the son he delights in.*

—Proverbs 3:11–12

*Train a child in the way he should go,
and when he is old he will not turn from it.*

—Proverbs 22:6

*Blessed is the man you discipline, O LORD,
the man you teach from your law;
you grant him relief from days of trouble,
till a pit is dug for the wicked.
For the LORD will not reject his people;
he will never forsake his inheritance.
Judgment will again be founded on righteousness,
and all the upright in heart will follow it.*

—Psalm 94:12–15

Week 11: Wednesday

Be self-controlled and alert.

—1 Peter 5:8

But the day of the Lord will come like a thief. The heavens will disappear with a roar; the elements will be destroyed by fire, and the earth and everything in it will be laid bare.
Since everything will be destroyed in this way, what kind of people ought you to be? You ought to live holy and godly lives as you look forward to the day of God and speed its coming. That day will bring about the destruction of the heavens by fire, and the elements will melt in the heat. But in keeping with his promise we are looking forward to a new heaven and a new earth, the home of righteousness.
So then, dear friends, since you are looking forward to this, make every effort to be found spotless, blameless and at peace with him.

—2 Peter 3:10–14

Guard what has been entrusted to your care.

—1 Timothy 6:20

Week 11: Thursday

Seek good, not evil,
that you may live.
*Then the L*ORD *God Almighty will be with you,*
just as you say he is.
Hate evil, love good;
maintain justice in the courts.

—Amos 5:14–15

He who heeds discipline shows the way to life,
but whoever ignores correction leads others
astray.

—Proverbs 10:17

He who ignores discipline despises himself,
but whoever heeds correction gains
understanding.

—Proverbs 15:32

Week 11: Friday

In your struggle against sin, you have not yet resisted to the point of shedding your blood. And you have forgotten that word of encouragement that addresses you as sons:

*"My son, do not make light of the Lord's discipline,
    and do not lose heart when he rebukes you,
because the Lord disciplines those he loves,
    and he punishes everyone he accepts as a son."*

Endure hardship as discipline; God is treating you as sons. For what son is not disciplined by his father? If you are not disciplined (and everyone undergoes discipline), then you are illegitimate children and not true sons. Moreover, we have all had human fathers who disciplined us and we respected them for it. How much more should we submit to the Father of our spirits and live! Our fathers disciplined us for a little while as they thought best; but God disciplines us for our good, that we may share in his holiness. No discipline seems pleasant at the time, but painful. Later on, however, it produces a harvest of righteousness and peace for those who have been trained by it.

—Hebrews 12:4–11

Week 11: Weekend

My son, keep your father's commands
and do not forsake your mother's teaching.
Bind them upon your heart forever;
fasten them around your neck.
When you walk, they will guide you;
when you sleep, they will watch over you;
when you awake, they will speak to you.
For these commands are a lamp,
this teaching is a light,
and the corrections of discipline
are the way to life.

—Proverbs 6:20–23

The LORD humbled you, causing you to hunger and then feeding you with manna, which neither you nor your fathers had known, to teach you that man does not live on bread alone but on every word that comes from the mouth of the LORD. Your clothes did not wear out and your feet did not swell during these forty years. Know then in your heart that as a man disciplines his son, so the LORD your God disciplines you.

—Deuteronomy 8:3–5

Week 12: Monday

Wisdom is supreme; therefore get wisdom.
Though it cost all you have, get understanding.
Esteem her, and she will exalt you;
embrace her, and she will honor you.
She will set a garland of grace on your head
and present you with a crown of splendor.

Listen, my son, accept what I say,
and the years of your life will be many.
I guide you in the way of wisdom
and lead you along straight paths.
When you walk, your steps will not be hampered;
when you run, you will not stumble.

—Proverbs 4:7–12

Understanding is a fountain of life to those who have it,
but folly brings punishment to fools.

—Proverbs 16:22

Week 12: Tuesday

Listen, my sons, to a father's instruction;
  pay attention and gain understanding.
I give you sound learning,
  so do not forsake my teaching.
When I was a boy in my father's house,
  still tender, and an only child of my mother,
he taught me and said,
  "Lay hold of my words with all your heart;
  keep my commands and you will live.
Get wisdom, get understanding;
  do not forget my words or swerve from them.
Do not forsake wisdom, and she will protect you;
  love her, and she will watch over you."

—Proverbs 4:1–6

I want to know Christ and the power of his resurrection and the fellowship of sharing in his sufferings, becoming like him in his death, and so, somehow, to attain to the resurrection from the dead.

—Philippians 3:10–11

Week 12: Wednesday

Does not wisdom call out?
    Does not understanding raise her voice?
On the heights along the way,
    where the paths meet, she takes her stand;
beside the gates leading into the city,
    at the entrances, she cries aloud:
"To you, O men, I call out;
    I raise my voice to all mankind.
You who are simple, gain prudence;
    you who are foolish, gain understanding.
Listen, for I have worthy things to say;
    I open my lips to speak what is right.
My mouth speaks with is true,
    for my lips detest wickedness.
All the words of my mouth are just;
    none of them is crooked or perverse.
To the discerning all of them are right;
    they are faultless to those who have knowledge.
Choose my instruction instead of silver,
    knowledge rather than choice gold,
for wisdom is more precious than rubies,
    and nothing you desire can compare with her."

—Proverbs 8:1–11

Week 12: Thursday

It is not good to have zeal without knowledge,
nor to be hasty and miss the way.

—Proverbs 19:2

He who pursues righteousness and love finds life,
prosperity and honor.

—Romans 10:1–2

And this is my prayer: that your love may abound more
and more in knowledge and depth of insight, so that
you may be able to discern what is best and may be
pure and blameless until the day of Christ, filled with
the fruit of righteousness that comes through Jesus
Christ—to the glory and praise of God.

—Philippians 1:9–11

Week 12: Friday

The law of the LORD is perfect,
reviving the soul.
The statutes of the LORD are trustworthy,
making wise the simple.
The precepts of the LORD are right,
giving joy to the heart.
The commands of the LORD are radiant,
giving light to the eyes.
The fear of the LORD is pure,
enduring forever.
The ordinances of the LORD are sure
and altogether righteous.
They are more precious than gold,
than much pure gold;
they are sweeter than honey,
than honey from the comb.
By them is your servant warned;
in keeping them there is great reward.

—Psalm 19:7–11

Week 12: Weekend

Moses said to the Israelites:
See, I have taught you decrees and laws as the LORD
my God commanded me, so that you may follow them
in the land you are entering to take possession of it.
Observe them carefully, for this will show your wisdom
and understanding to the nations, who will hear about
all these decrees and say, "Surely this great nation is a
wise and understanding people." What other nation is
so great as to have their gods near them the way the
LORD our God is near us whenever we pray to him? And
what other nation is so great as to have such righteous
decrees and laws as this body of laws I am setting
before you today?
Only be careful, and watch yourselves closely so that
you do not forget the things your eyes have seen or let
them slip from your heart as long as you live. Teach
them to your children and to their children after them.

—*Deuteronomy 4:5–9*

*The law from your mouth is more precious to me
than thousands of pieces of silver and gold.*

—*Psalm 119:72*

Week 13: Monday

Jesus said,
"You have heard that it was said to the people long ago,
'Do not murder, and anyone who murders will be subject to judgment.' But I tell you that anyone who is
angry with his brother will be subject to judgment.
Again, anyone who says to his brother, 'Raca,' is
answerable to the Sanhedrin. But anyone who says,
'You fool!' will be in danger of the fire of hell.
"Therefore if you are offering your gift at the altar and
there remember that your brother has something
against you, leave your gift there in front of the altar.
First go and be reconciled to your brother; then come
and offer your gift."

—Matthew 5:21–24

Let no debt remain outstanding, except the continuing
debt to love one another, for he who loves his fellowman has fulfilled the law. The commandments, "Do not
commit adultery," "Do not murder," "Do not steal," "Do
not covet," and whatever other commandment there
may be, are summed up in this one rule: "Love your
neighbor as yourself." Love does no harm to its neighbor. Therefore, love is the fulfillment of the law.

—Romans 13:8–10

Week 13: Tuesday

An angry man stirs up dissension,
and a hot-tempered one commits many sins.

—Proverbs 29:22

Jesus said,
"You have heard that it was said, 'Eye for eye, and tooth for tooth.' But I tell you, Do not resist an evil person. If someone strikes you on the right cheek, turn to him the other also. And if someone wants to sue you and take your tunic, let him have your cloak as well. If someone forces you to go one mile, go with him two miles. Give to the one who asks you, and do not turn away from the one who wants to borrow from you."

—Matthew 5:38–42

A man's wisdom gives him patience;
it is to his glory to overlook an offense.

—Proverbs 19:11

Week 13: Wednesday

What causes fights and quarrels among you? Don't they come from your desires that battle within you? You want something but don't get it. You kill and covet, but you cannot have what you want. You quarrel and fight. You do not have, because you do not ask God.

—*James 4:1–2*

A greedy man stirs up dissension,
but he who trusts in the LORD will prosper.

—**Proverbs 28:25**

Judgment without mercy will be shown to anyone who has not been merciful. Mercy triumphs over judgment!

—*James 2:13*

It is to a man's honor to avoid strife,
but every fool is quick to quarrel.

—**Proverbs 20:3**

Week 13: Thursday

There are six things the LORD hates,
seven that are detestable to him:
haughty eyes,
a lying tongue,
hands that shed innocent blood,
a heart that devises wicked schemes,
feet that are quick to rush into evil,
a false witness who pours out lies
and a man who stirs up dissension among
brothers.

—Proverbs 6:16–19

Hatred stirs up dissension,
but love covers over all wrongs.

—Proverbs 10:12

In your anger do not sin;
when you are on your beds,
search your hearts and be silent.

—Psalm 4:4

Blessed are the peacemakers,
for they will be called sons of God.

—Matthew 5:9

Week 13: Friday

Jesus said,
"You have heard that it was said, 'Love your neighbor and hate your enemy.' But I tell you: Love your enemies and pray for those who persecute you, that you may be sons of your Father in heaven. He causes his sun to rise on the evil and the good, and sends rain on the righteous and the unrighteous. If you love those who love you, what reward will you get? Are not even the tax collectors doing that? And if you greet only your brothers, what are you doing more than others? Do not even pagans do that? Be perfect, therefore, as your heavenly Father is perfect."

—*Matthew 5:43–48*

May the God who gives endurance and encouragement give you a spirit of unity among yourselves as you follow Christ Jesus, so that with one heart and mouth you may glorify the God and Father of our Lord Jesus Christ.

—*Romans 15:5–6*

When a man's ways are pleasing to the LORD,
*   he makes even his enemies live at peace with him.*

—*Proverbs 16:7*

Week 13: Weekend

Do not repay anyone evil for evil. Be careful to do what is right in the eyes of everybody. If it is possible, as far as it depends on you, live at peace with everyone. Do not take revenge, my friends, but leave room for God's wrath, for it is written: "It is mine to avenge; I will repay," says the Lord. On the contrary:

"If your enemy is hungry, feed him;
if he is thirsty, give him something to drink.
In doing this, you will heap burning coals on his head."

Do not be overcome by evil, but overcome evil with good.

—Romans 12:17–21

The teaching of the wise is a fountain of life,
turning a man from the snares of death.

—Proverbs 13:14

Week 14: Monday

A friend loves at all times,
*   and a brother is born for adversity.*

—Proverbs 17:17

Two are better than one,
*   because they have a good return for their work:*
If one falls down,
*   his friend can help him up.*
But pity the man who falls
*   and has no one to help him up!*
Also, if two lie down together, they will keep warm.
*   But how can one keep warm alone?*
Though one may be overpowered,
*   two can defend themselves.*
A cord of three strands is not quickly broken.

—Ecclesiastes 4:9–12

Jesus replied, "If anyone loves me, he will obey my teaching. My Father will love him, and we will come to him and make our home with him."

—John 14:23

Week 14: Tuesday

He who walks with the wise grows wise,
  but a companion of fools suffers harm.

—Proverbs 13:20

Do not be misled: "Bad company corrupts good
character."

—1 Corinthians 15:33

Above all, love each other deeply, because love covers
over a multitude of sins.

—1 Peter 4:8

I am a friend to all who fear you, LORD,
  to all who follow your precepts.

—Psalm 119:63

Week 14: Wednesday

Listen to my prayer, O God,
do not ignore my plea;
hear me and answer me.
My thoughts trouble me and I am distraught

If an enemy were insulting me,
I could endure it;
if a foe were raising himself against me,
I could hide from him.
But it is you, a man like myself,
my companion, my close friend,
with whom I once enjoyed sweet fellowship
as we walked with the throng at the house of God.

—Psalm 55:1–2, 12–14

I no longer call you servants, because a servant does not know his master's business. Instead, I have called you friends, for everything that I learned from my Father I have made known to you.

—John 15:15

Week 14: Thursday

Do not make friends with a hot-tempered man,
  do not associate with one easily angered,
or you may learn his ways
  and get yourself ensnared.

—*Proverbs 22:24–25*

A man of many companions may come to ruin,
  but there is a friend who sticks closer than a
  brother.

—*Proverbs 18:24*

The LORD does not look at the things man looks at. Man looks at the outward appearance, but the LORD looks at the heart.

—*1 Samuel 16:7*

Stay away from a foolish man,
  for you will not find knowledge on his lips.

—*Proverbs 14:7*

Week 14: Friday

Dear friends, let us love one another, for love comes from God. Everyone who loves has been born of God and knows God. Whoever does not love does not know God, because God is love. This is how God showed his love among us: He sent his one and only son into the world that we might live through him. This is love: not that we loved God, but that he loved us and sent his Son as an atoning sacrifice for our sins. Dear friends, since God so loved us, we also ought to love one another.

—*1 John 4:7–11*

A righteous man is cautious in friendship,
but the way of the wicked leads them astray.

—**Proverbs 12:26**

Week 14: Weekend

Do not envy wicked men,
do not desire their company;
for their hearts plot violence,
and their lips talk about making trouble.

—Proverbs 24:1–2

As for those who seemed to be important—whatever they were makes no difference to me; God does not judge by external appearance.

—Galatians 2:6

It was good of you to share in my troubles. ... And my God will meet all your needs according to his glorious riches in Christ Jesus.

—Philippians 4:14, 19

Week 15: Monday

Teach me, O LORD, to follow your decrees;
  then I will keep them to the end.
Give me understanding, and I will keep your law
  and obey it with all my heart.
Direct me in the path of your commands,
  for there I find delight.
Turn my heart toward your statutes
  and not toward selfish gain.
Turn my eyes away from worthless things;
  preserve my life according to your word.
Fulfill your promise to your servant,
  so that you may be feared.
Take away the disgrace I dread,
  for your laws are good.
How I long for your precepts!
  Preserve my life in your righteousness. . . .

Do good to your servant
  according to your word, O LORD.
Teach me knowledge and good judgment,
  for I believe in your commands.

—Psalm 119:33–40, 65–66

Week 15: Tuesday

The fear of the LORD is the beginning of knowledge.
—Proverbs 1:7

*The eyes of the LORD keep watch over knowledge,
but he frustrates the words of the unfaithful.*

—Proverbs 22:12

*Praise be to the name of God for ever and ever;
wisdom and power are his.
He changes times and seasons;
he sets up kings and deposes them.
He gives wisdom to the wise
and knowledge to the discerning.
He reveals deep and hidden things;
he knows what lies in darkness,
and light dwells with him.*

—Daniel 2:20–22

Week 15: Wednesday

My son, if you accept my words
and store up my commands within you,
turning your ear to wisdom
and applying your heart to understanding,
and if you call out for insight
and cry aloud for understanding,
and if you look for it as for silver
and search for it as for hidden treasure,
then you will understand the fear of the LORD
and find the knowledge of God.
For the LORD gives wisdom,
and from his mouth come knowledge and
understanding.

—Proverbs 2:1–6

Since the day we heard about you, we have not
stopped praying for you and asking God to fill you with
the knowledge of his will through all spiritual wisdom
and understanding.

—Colossians 1:9

It is the spirit in a man,
the breath of the Almighty,
that gives him understanding.

—Job 32:8

Week 15: Thursday

The fear of the LORD is the beginning of wisdom;
  all who follow his precepts have good
  understanding.
  To him belongs eternal praise.

—Psalm 111:10

The heavens declare the glory of God;
  the skies proclaim the work of his hands.
Day after day they pour forth speech;
  night after night they display knowledge.
There is no speech or language
  where their voice is not heard.
Their voice goes out into all the earth,
  their words to the ends of the world.

—Psalm 19:1–4

Who has understood the mind of the LORD,
  or instructed him as his counselor?
Whom did the LORD consult to enlighten him,
  and who taught him the right way?
Who was it that taught him knowledge
  or showed him the path of understanding?

—Isaiah 40:13–14

Week 15: Friday

Jesus said,
"The knowledge of the secrets of the kingdom of heaven has been given to you, but not to them. Whoever has will be given more, and he will have an abundance. Whoever does not have, even what he has will be taken from him. This is why I speak to them in parables:

'Though seeing, they do not see;
though hearing, they do not hear or understand.

In them is fulfilled the prophecy of Isaiah:

" 'You will be ever hearing but never understanding;
you will be ever seeing but never perceiving.
For this people's heart has become calloused;
they hardly hear with their ears,
and they have closed their eyes.
Otherwise they might see with their eyes,
hear with their ears,
understand with their hearts
and turn, and I would heal them.'

But blessed are your eyes because they see, and your ears because they hear."

—Matthew 13:11–16

Week 15: **Weekend**

My purpose is that [the believers] may be encouraged in heart and united in love, so that they may have the full riches of complete understanding, in order that they may know the mystery of God, namely, Christ, in whom are hidden all the treasures of wisdom and knowledge.

—*Colossians 2:2–3*

*O LORD, you have searched me
    and you know me.
You know when I sit and when I rise;
    you perceive my thoughts from afar.
You discern my going out and my lying down;
    you are familiar with all my ways.
Before a word is on my tongue
    you know it completely, O LORD.*

*You hem me in—behind and before;
    you have laid your hand upon me.
Such knowledge is too wonderful for me,
    too lofty for me to attain.*

—*Psalm 139:1–6*

Week 16: Monday

Hasten, O God, to save me;
O Lord, come quickly to help me.

May those who seek my life
be put to shame and confusion;

may all who desire my ruin
be turned back in disgrace.

May those who say to me, "Aha! Aha!"
turn back because of their shame.

But may all who seek you
rejoice and be glad in you;

may those who love your salvation always say,
"Let God be exalted!"

Yet I am poor and needy;
come quickly to me, O God.

You are my help and my deliverer;
O Lord, do not delay.

—*Psalm 70*

Week 16: Tuesday

And you will know that I have sent you this admonition so that my covenant with Levi may continue," says the LORD Almighty. "My covenant was with him, a covenant of life and peace, and I gave them to him; this called for reverence and he revered me and stood in awe of my name. True instruction was in his mouth and nothing false was found on his lips. He walked with me in peace and uprightness, and turned many from sin. "For the lips of a priest ought to preserve knowledge, and from his mouth men should seek instruction—because he is the messenger of the LORD Almighty. But you have turned from the way and by your teaching have caused many to stumble; you have violated the covenant with Levi," says the LORD Almighty. "So I have caused you to be despised and humiliated before all the people, because you have not followed my ways but have shown partiality in matters of the law."

—*Malachi 2:4–9*

He will deliver the needy who cry out, the afflicted who have no one to help.

—*Psalm 72:12*

Week 16: Wednesday

Because he himself suffered when he was tempted, he
is able to help those who are being tempted.

—Hebrews 2:18

You, O God, do see trouble and grief;
*   you consider it to take it in hand.*
The victim commits himself to you;
*   you are the helper of the fatherless.*

—Psalm 10:14

Surely the arm of the LORD is not too short to save, nor
his ear too dull to hear.

—Isaiah 59:1

Week 16: Thursday

Wisdom has built her house;
*   has hewn out its seven pillars.*
She has prepared her meat and mixed her wine;
*   has also set her table.*
She has sent out her maids, and she calls
*   from the highest point of the city.*
"Let all who are simple come in here!"
*   she says to those who lack judgment.*
"Come, eat my food
*   and drink the wine I have mixed.*
Leave your simple ways and you will live;
*   walk in the way of understanding."*

—Proverbs 9:1–6

I have kept my feet from every evil path
*   so that I might obey your word.*
I have not departed from your laws,
*   for you yourself have taught me.*
How sweet are your words to my taste,
*   sweeter than honey to my mouth!*
I gain understanding from your precepts;
*   therefore I hate every wrong path.*

—Psalm 119:101–104

Week 16: Friday

All your commands are trustworthy;
help me, for men persecute me without cause.
They almost wiped me from the earth,
but I have not forsaken your precepts.
Preserve my life according to your love,
and I will obey the statutes of your mouth.

—**Psalm 119:86–88**

God is our refuge and strength,
an ever-present help in trouble.

—**Psalm 46:1**

It is the Sovereign LORD who helps me. Who is he that will condemn me?

—**Isaiah 50:9**

Week 16: Weekend

Do good to your servant, and I will live;
I will obey your word.
Open my eyes that I may see
wonderful things in your law.
I am a stranger on earth;
do not hide your commands from me.
My soul is consumed with longing
for your laws at all times.
You rebuke the arrogant, who are cursed
and who stray from your commands.
Remove from me scorn and contempt,
for I keep your statutes.
Though rulers sit together and slander me,
your servant will meditate on your decrees.
Your statutes are my delight;
they are my counselors.

—Psalm 119:17–24

So we way with confidence,
"The Lord is my helper;
I will not be afraid.
What can man do to me?"

—Hebrews 13:6

Week 17: Monday

Let us fix our eyes on Jesus, the author and perfecter of our faith, who for the joy set before him endured the cross, scorning its shame, and sat down at the right hand of the throne of God. Consider him who endured such opposition from sinful men, so that you will not grow weary and lose heart.

—Hebrews 12:2–3

Jesus said,
"I am the vine; you are the branches. If a man remains in me and I in him, he will bear much fruit; apart from me you can do nothing. If anyone does not remain in me, he is like a branch that is thrown away and withers; such branches are picked up, thrown into the fire and burned. If you remain in me and my words remain in you, ask whatever you wish, and it will be given you. This is to my Father's glory, that you bear much fruit, showing yourselves to be my disciples."

—John 15:5–8

Week 17: Tuesday

Since, then, you have been raised with Christ, set your hearts on things above, where Christ is seated at the right hand of God. Set your minds on things above, not on earthly things.

—Colossians 3:1–2

Whatever is true, whatever is noble, whatever is right, whatever is pure, whatever is lovely, whatever is admirable—if anything is excellent or praiseworthy—think about such things.

—Philippians 4:8

My eyes are fixed on you, O Sovereign LORD;
in you I take refuge.

—Psalm 141:8

Week 17: Wednesday

Surely you desire truth in the inner parts;
*   you teach me wisdom in the inmost place.*
Cleanse me with hyssop, and I will be clean;
*   wash me, and I will be whiter than snow.*
Create in me a pure heart, O God,
*   and renew a steadfast spirit within me.*
Do not cast me from your presence
*   or take your Holy Spirit from me.*
Restore to me the joy of your salvation
*   and grant me a willing spirit, to sustain me.*

—Psalm 51:6–7, 10–12

A discerning man keeps wisdom in view,
*   but a fool's eyes wander to the ends of the earth.*

—Proverbs 17:24

Week 17: Thursday

Let your eyes look straight ahead,
fix your gaze directly before you.
Make level paths for your feet
and take only ways that are firm.
Do not swerve to the right or the left;
keep your foot from evil.

—Proverbs 4:25–27

Great peace have they who love your law,
and nothing can make them stumble.

—Psalm 119:165

The worries of this life and the deceitfulness of
wealth choke [the message of the kingdom], making it
unfruitful.

—Matthew 13:22

Week 17: Friday

I do not consider myself yet to have taken hold of it. But one thing I do: Forgetting what is behind and straining toward what is ahead, I press on toward the goal to win the prize for which God has called me heavenward in Christ Jesus.

—Philippians 3:13–14

I press on to take hold of that for which Christ Jesus took hold of me. Brothers, I do not consider myself yet to have taken hold of it. But one thing I do: Forgetting what is behind and straining toward what is ahead, I press on toward the goal to win the prize for which God has called me heavenward in Christ Jesus.

—Philippians 3:12–14

Week 17: Weekend

*You will keep in perfect peace
   him whose mind is steadfast,
   because he trusts in you.
Trust in the LORD forever,
   for the LORD, the LORD, is the Rock eternal.*

—*Isaiah 26:3–4*

As Jesus and his disciples were on their way, he came to a village where a woman named Martha opened her home to him. She had a sister called Mary, who sat at the Lord's feet listening to what he said. But Martha was distracted by all the preparations that had to be made. She came to him and asked, "Lord, don't you care that my sister has left me to do the work by myself? Tell her to help me!"

"Martha, Martha," the Lord answered, "you are worried and upset about many things, but only one thing is needed. Mary has chosen what is better, and it will not be taken away from her."

—*Luke 10:38–42*

Week 18: Monday

Encourage the young men to be self-controlled. In everything set them an example by doing what is good. In your teaching show integrity, seriousness and soundness of speech that cannot be condemned, so that those who oppose you may be ashamed because they have nothing bad to say.

—Titus 2:6–8

Be prepared in season and out of season; correct, rebuke and encourage—with great patience and careful instruction.

—2 Timothy 4:2

Be shepherds of God's flock that is under your care, . . . not lording it over those entrusted to you, but being examples to the flock.

—1 Peter 5:2–3

Week 18: Tuesday

For you were once darkness, but now you are light in the Lord. Live as children of light (for the fruit of the light consists in all goodness, righteousness and truth) and find out what pleases the Lord.

—Ephesians 5:8–10

If you make the Most High your dwelling—
*   even the LORD, who is my refuge—*
then no harm will befall you,
*   no disaster will come near your tent.*
For he will command his angels concerning you
*   to guard you in all your ways;*
they will lift you up in their hands,
*   so that you will not strike your foot against a stone.*

—Psalm 91:9–12

Week 18: Wednesday

Put to death, therefore, whatever belongs to your earthly nature: sexual immorality, impurity, lust, evil desires and greed, which is idolatry. Because of these, the wrath of God is coming. You used to walk in these ways, in the life you once lived. But now you must rid yourselves of all such things as these: anger, rage, malice, slander, and filthy language from your lips. Do not lie to each other, since you have taken off your old self with its practices and have put on the new self, which is being renewed in knowledge in the image of its Creator. Here there is no Greek or Jew, circumcised or uncircumcised, barbarian, Scythian, slave or free, but Christ is all, and is in all.

Therefore, as God's chosen people, holy and dearly loved, clothe yourselves with compassion, kindness, humility, gentleness and patience. Bear with each other and forgive whatever grievances you may have against one another. Forgive as the Lord forgave you. And over all these virtues put on love, which binds them all together in perfect unity.

—*Colossians 3:5–14*

Week 18: Thursday

But you, man of God, flee from all this, and pursue righteousness, godliness, faith, love, endurance and gentleness. Fight the good fight of the faith. Take hold of the eternal life to which you were called when you made your good confession in the presence of many witnesses.

—*1 Timothy 6:11–12*

Greater love has no one than this, that he lay down his life for his friends.

—*John 15:13*

Week 18: Friday

For the grace of God that brings salvation has appeared to all men. It teaches us to say "No" to ungodliness and worldly passions, and to live self-controlled, upright and godly lives in this present age, while we wait for the blessed hope—the glorious appearing of our great God and Savior, Jesus Christ.

—*Titus 2:11–13*

The hour has come for you to wake up from your slumber, because our salvation is nearer now than when we first believed. The night is nearly over; the day is almost here. So let us put aside the deeds of darkness and put on the armor of light. Let us behave decently, as in the daytime. . . . Rather, clothe yourselves with the Lord Jesus Christ, and do not think about how to gratify the desires of the sinful nature.

—*Romans 13:11–14*

Week 18: Weekend

Above all, my brothers, do not swear—not by heaven or by earth or by anything else. Let your "Yes" be yes, and your "No," no, or you will be condemned.

—James 5:12

Come, my children, listen to me;
I will teach you the fear of the LORD.
Whoever of you loves life
and desires to see many good days,
keep your tongue from evil
and your lips from speaking lies.
Turn from evil and do good;
seek peace and pursue it.

—Psalm 34:11–14

Don't let anyone look down on you because you are young, but set an example for the believers in speech, in life, in love, in faith and in purity.

—1 Timothy 4:12

Week 19: Monday

Lord, you have been our dwelling place
throughout all generations.
Before the mountains were born
or you brought forth the earth and the world,
from everlasting to everlasting you are God. . . .

For a thousand years in your sight
are like a day that has just gone by,
or like a watch in the night ...
Teach us to number our days aright,
that we may gain a heart of wisdom.

—Psalm 90:1-2, 4, 12

Week 19: Tuesday

The fear of the LORD is the beginning of wisdom,
    and knowledge of the Holy One is
    understanding.
For through me your days will be many,
    and years will be added to your life.

—Proverbs 9:10–11

Now all has been heard;
    here is the conclusion of the matter:
Fear God and keep his commandments,
    for this is the whole duty of man.

—Ecclesiastes 12:13

Week 19: Wednesday

O LORD, the king rejoices in your strength.
How great is his joy in the victories you give!
You have granted him the desire of his heart
and have not withheld the request of his lips.

You welcomed him with rich blessings
and placed a crown of pure gold on his head.
He asked you for life, and you gave it to him—
length of days, for ever and ever.

—Psalm 21:1–4

The wise heart will know the proper time and procedure. For there is a proper time and procedure for every matter.

—Ecclesiastes 8:5–6

God is our God for ever and ever;
he will be our guide even to the end.

—Psalm 48:14

Week 19: Thursday

Show me, O LORD, my life's end
and the number of my days;
let me know how fleeting is my life.
You have made my days a mere handbreadth;
the span of my years is as nothing before you.
Each man's life is but a breath.
Man is a mere phantom as he goes to and fro:
He bustles about, but only in vain;
he heaps up wealth, not knowing who will get it.

But now, Lord, what do I look for?
My hope is in you.

—Psalm 39:4–7

Week 19: Friday

There is a time for everything,
and a season for every activity under heaven:

a time to be born and a time to die,
a time to plant and a time to uproot,
a time to kill and a time to heal,
a time to tear down and a time to build,
a time to weep and a time to laugh,
a time to mourn and a time to dance,
a time to scatter stones and a time to gather them,
a time to embrace and a time to refrain,
a time to search and a time to give up,
a time to keep and a time to throw away,
a time to tear and a time to mend,
a time to be silent and a time to speak,
a time to love and a time to hate,
a time for war and a time for peace.

—Ecclesiastes 3:1–8

Week 19: Weekend

Fix these words of mine in your hearts and minds; tie them as symbols on your hands and bind them on your foreheads. Teach them to your children, talking about them when you sit at home and when you walk along the road, when you lie down and when you get up. Write them on the doorframes of your houses and on your gates, so that your days and the days of your children may be many in the land that the LORD swore to give your forefathers, as many as the days that the heavens are above the earth.

—Deuteronomy 11:18–21

O LORD, what is man that you care for him,
*   the son of man that you think of him?*
Man is like a breath;
*   his days are like a fleeting shadow.*

—Psalm 144:3–4

Week 20: Monday

Cast your cares on the LORD
and he will sustain you;
he will never let the righteous fall.

—Psalm 55:22

Jesus said,
"Do not let your hearts be troubled. Trust in God; trust
also in me."

—John 14:1

If the LORD delights in a man's way,
he makes his steps firm;
though he stumble, he will not fall,
for the LORD upholds him with his hand.

I was young and now I am old,
yet I have never seen the righteous forsaken
or their children begging bread.
They are always generous and lend freely;
their children will be blessed.

—Psalm 37:23–26

Week 20: Tuesday

Jesus said to his disciples: "Therefore I tell you, do not worry about your life, what you will eat; or about your body, what you will wear. Life is more than food, and the body more than clothes. Consider the ravens: They do not sow or reap, they have no storeroom or barn; yet God feeds them. And how much more valuable you are than birds! Who of you by worrying can add a single hour to his life? Since you cannot do this very little thing, why do you worry about the rest? "Consider how the lilies grow. They do not labor or spin. Yet I tell you, not even Solomon in all his splendor was dressed like one of these. If that is how God clothes the grass of the field, which is here today, and tomorrow is thrown into the fire, how much more will he clothe you, O you of little faith! And do not set your heart on what you will eat or drink; do not worry about it. For the pagan world runs after all such things, and your Father knows that you need them. But seek his kingdom, and these things will be given to you as well.

—Luke 12:22–31

Week 20: **Wednesday**

*"Though the mountains be shaken
    and the hills be removed,
yet my unfailing love for you will not be shaken
    nor my covenant of peace be removed,"
    says the Lord, who has compassion on you.*

—**Isaiah 54:10**

*But blessed is the man who trusts in the Lord,
    whose confidence is in him.
He will be like a tree planted by the water
    that sends out its roots by the stream.
It does not fear when heat comes;
    its leaves are always green.
It has no worries in a year of drought
    and never fails to bear fruit.*

—**Jeremiah 17:7–8**

Week 20: Thursday

The LORD is gracious and compassionate,
slow to anger and rich in love.
The LORD is good to all;
he has compassion on all he has made.
All you have made will praise you, O LORD;
your saints will extol you.
They will tell of the glory of your kingdom
and speak of your might,
so that all men may know of your mighty acts
and the glorious splendor of your kingdom.
Your kingdom is an everlasting kingdom,
and your dominion endures through
all generations.

The LORD is faithful to all his promises
and loving toward all he has made.
The LORD upholds all those who fall
and lifts up all who are bowed down.
The eyes of all look to you,
and you give them their food at the proper time.
You open your hand
and satisfy the desires of every living thing.

—Psalm 145:8–16

Week 20: Friday

Have no fear of sudden disaster
*   or of the ruin that overtakes the wicked,*
for the LORD will be your confidence
*   and will keep your foot from being snared.*

—Proverbs 3:25–26

"Because he loves me," says the LORD, "I will rescue
him;
*   I will protect him, for he acknowledges my name.*
He will call upon me, and I will answer him;
*   I will be with him in trouble,*
*   I will deliver him and honor him.*
With long life will I satisfy him
*   and show him my salvation."*

—Psalm 91:14–16

The LORD gives strength to his people;
*   the LORD blesses his people with peace.*

—Psalm 29:11

Week 20: Weekend

God is our refuge and strength,
    an ever-present help in trouble.
Therefore we will not fear, though the earth give way
    and the mountains fall into the heart of the sea,
though its waters roar and foam
    and the mountains quake with their surging. . . .

Come and see the works of the LORD,
    the desolations he has brought on the earth.
He makes wars cease to the ends of the earth;
    he breaks the bow and shatters the spear,
    he burns the shields with fire.

"Be still, and know that I am God;
    I will be exalted among the nations,
    I will be exalted in the earth."

The LORD Almighty is with us;
    the God of Jacob is our fortress.

—Psalm 46:1–3, 8–11

Week 21: Monday

Taste and see that the LORD is good;
*   blessed is the man who takes refuge in him.*
Fear the LORD, you his saints,
*   for those who fear him lack nothing.*
The lions may grow weak and hungry,
*   but those who seek the LORD lack no good thing.*

—Psalm 34:8–10

May God give you the desire of your heart
*   and make all your plans succeed.*
We will shout for joy when you are victorious
*   and will lift up our banners in the name of our God.*
May the LORD grant all your requests.

—Psalm 20:4–5

There is no wisdom, no insight, no plan
*   that can succeed against the LORD.*

—Proverbs 21:30

Week 21: Tuesday

He who gets wisdom loves his own soul;
*   he who cherishes understanding prospers.*

—Proverbs 19:8

While Joseph was there in the prison, the LORD was
with him; he showed him kindness and granted him
favor in the eyes of the prison warden. So the warden
put Joseph in charge of all those held in the prison,
and he was made responsible for all that was done
there. The warden paid no attention to anything under
Joseph's care, because the LORD was with Joseph and
gave him success in whatever he did.

—Genesis 39:20–23

Success, success to you,
*   and success to those who help you,*
*   for your God will help you.*

—1 Chronicles 12:18

Commit to the LORD whatever you do,
*   and your plans will succeed.*

—Proverbs 16:3

Week 21: Wednesday

Whoever gives heed to instruction prospers,
*   and blessed is he who trusts in the LORD.*

—Proverbs 16:20

Plans fail for lack of counsel,
*   but with many advisers they succeed.*

—Proverbs 15:22

"Be strong and courageous, because you will lead
these people to inherit the land I swore to their
forefathers to give them. Be strong and very courageous. Be careful to obey all the law my servant
Moses gave you; do not turn from it to the right or to
the left, that you may be successful wherever you go.
Do not let this Book of the Law depart from your mouth;
meditate on it day and night, so that you may be careful to do everything written in it. Then you will be pros-
perous and successful. Have I not commanded you?
Be strong and courageous. Do not be terrified; do not
be discouraged, for the LORD your God will be with you
wherever you go."

—Joshua 1:6–9

Week 21: Thursday

He [who delights in the law of the LORD] is like a tree
planted by streams of water,
    which yields its fruit in season
and whose leaf does not wither.
    Whatever he does prospers.

—*Psalm 1:3*

In everything he did David had great success, because
the LORD was with him.

—*1 Samuel 18:14*

The path of the righteous is level;
    O upright One, you make the way of the righteous
    smooth.
Yes, LORD, walking in the way of your laws,
    we wait for you;
your name and renown
    are the desire of our hearts.
My soul yearns for you in the night;
    in the morning my spirit longs for you. . . .

LORD, you establish peace for us;
    all that we have accomplished you have done
    for us.

—*Isaiah 26:7–9, 12*

Week 21: Friday

Do not fret because of evil men
*   or be envious of those who do wrong;*
for like the grass they will soon wither,
*   like green plants they will soon die away.*

Trust in the Lord and do good;
*   dwell in the land and enjoy safe pasture.*
Delight yourself in the Lord
*   and he will give you the desires of your heart.*

—Psalm 37:1–4

Uzziah was sixteen years old when he became king, and he reigned in Jerusalem fifty-two years. . . . He did what was right in the eyes of the Lord, just as his father Amaziah had done. He sought God during the days of Zechariah, who instructed him in the fear of God. As long as he sought the Lord, God gave him success.

—2 Chronicles 26:3–5

Week 21: Weekend

Some men came and told Jehoshaphat, "A vast army is coming against you." . . . Alarmed, Jehoshaphat resolved to inquire of the LORD, and he proclaimed a fast for all Judah. The people of Judah came together to seek help from the LORD; indeed, they came from every town in Judah to seek him.

All the men of Judah, with their wives and children and little ones, stood there before the LORD.

Jehoshaphat bowed with his face to the ground, and all the people of Judah and Jerusalem fell down in worship before the LORD.

Early in the morning they left for the Desert of Tekoa. As they set out, Jehoshaphat stood and said, "Listen to me, Judah and people of Jerusalem! Have faith in the LORD your God and you will be upheld; have faith in his prophets and you will be successful." After consulting the people, Jehoshaphat appointed men to sing to the LORD and to praise him for the splendor of his holiness. . . .

As they began to sing and praise, the LORD set ambushes against the men of Ammon and Moab and Mount Seir who were invading Judah, and they were defeated.

—2 Chronicles 20:2-4, 13, 18, 20-22

Week 22: Monday

We do not lose heart. Though outwardly we are wasting away, yet inwardly we are being renewed day by day. For our light and momentary troubles are achieving for us an eternal glory that far outweighs them all. So we fix our eyes not on what is seen, but on what is unseen. For what is seen is temporary, but what is unseen is eternal.

—2 Corinthians 4:16–18

Commit your way to the LORD;
*   trust in him and he will do this:*
He will make your righteousness shine like the dawn,
*   the justice of your cause like the noonday sun.*

Be still before the LORD and wait patiently for him;
*   do not fret when men succeed in their ways,*
*   when they carry out their wicked schemes.*

—Psalm 37:5–7

Week 22: Tuesday

To you, O Lord, I lift up my soul;
in you I trust, O my God.
Do not let me be put to shame,
nor let my enemies triumph over me.
No one whose hope is in you
will ever be put to shame, . . .

Show me your ways, O Lord,
teach me your paths;
guide me in your truth and teach me,
for you are God my Savior,
and my hope is in you all day long.

—Psalm 25:1–5

Though you have made me see troubles,
many and bitter, Lord,
you will restore my life again;
from the depths of the earth
you will again bring me up.
You will increase my honor
and comfort me once again.

—Psalm 71:20–21

Week 22: Wednesday

Have mercy on me, O God,
*   according to your unfailing love;*
according to your great compassion
*   blot out my transgressions.*
Wash away all my iniquity
*   and cleanse me from my sin. . . .*

Cleanse me with hyssop, and I will be clean;
*   wash me, and I will be whiter than snow.*
Let me hear joy and gladness;
*   let the bones you have crushed rejoice.*
Hide your face from my sins
*   and blot out all my iniquity.*

Create in me a pure heart, O God,
*   and renew a steadfast spirit within me.*
Do not cast me from your presence
*   or take your Holy Spirit from me.*
Restore to me the joy of your salvation
*   and grant me a willing spirit, to sustain me.*

—Psalm 51:1–2, 7–12

Week 22: Thursday

The LORD is my shepherd, I shall not be in want.
He makes me lie down in green pastures,
he leads me beside quiet waters,
he restores my soul.
He guides me in paths of righteousness
for his name's sake.
Even though I walk
through the valley of the shadow of death,
I will fear no evil,
for you are with me;
your rod and your staff,
they comfort me.

You prepare a table before me
in the presence of my enemies.
You anoint my head with oil;
my cup overflows.
Surely goodness and love will follow me
all the days of my life,
and I will dwell in the house of the LORD
forever.

—Psalm 23

Week 22: Friday

I am still confident of this:
I will see the goodness of the LORD
in the land of the living.
Wait for the LORD;
be strong and take heart
and wait for the LORD.

—**Psalm 27:13–14**

How many are your works, O LORD!
In wisdom you made them all;
the earth is full of your creatures.
There is the sea, vast and spacious,
teeming with creatures beyond number—
living things both large and small.

These all look to you
to give them their food at the proper time.
When you give it to them,
they gather it up;
when you open your hand,
they are satisfied with good things.
When you send your Spirit,
they are created,
and you renew the face of the earth.

—**Psalm 104: 24-25, 27-28, 30**

Week 22: Weekend

*Because of the L*ORD*'s great love we are not consumed,*
for his compassions never fail.
They are new every morning;
great is your faithfulness.
*I say to myself, "The L*ORD *is my portion;*
therefore I will wait for him."

*The L*ORD *is good to those whose hope is in him,*
to the one who seeks him;
it is good to wait quietly
*for the salvation of the L*ORD*.*

—Lamentations 3:22–26

Why are you downcast, O my soul?
Why so disturbed within me?
Put your hope in God,
for I will yet praise him,
my Savior and my God.

—Psalm 42:11

Week 23: Monday

Jesus said,
"A man going on a journey . . . called his servants and
entrusted his property to them. To one he gave five talents of money, to another two talents, and to another
one talent, each according to his ability. Then he went
on his journey. The man who had received the five talents went at once and put his money to work and
gained five more. . . .
"After a long time the master of those servants
returned and settled accounts with them. The man who
had received the five talents brought the other five.
'Master,' he said, 'you entrusted me with five talents.
See, I have gained five more.'
"His master replied, 'Well done, good and faithful servant! You have been faithful with a few things; I will put
you in charge of many things. Come and share your
master's happiness!'. . .
For everyone who has will be given more, and he will
have an abundance.

—*Matthew 25:14–16, 19–21, 29*

Week 23: Tuesday

Sing joyfully to the LORD, you righteous;
it is fitting for the upright to praise him.
Praise the LORD with the harp;
make music to him on the ten-stringed lyre.
Sing to him a new song;
play skillfully, and shout for joy.

—*Psalm 33:1–3*

As for Jeduthun, from his sons: Gedaliah, Zeri, Jeshaiah, Shimei, Hashabiah and Mattithiah, six in all, under the supervision of their father Jeduthun, who prophesied, using the harp in thanking and praising the LORD.

—*1 Chronicles 25:3*

My heart is steadfast, O God;
I will sing and make music with all my soul.
Awake, harp and lyre!
I will awaken the dawn.
I will praise you, O LORD, among the nations;
I will sing of you among the peoples.
For great is your love, higher than the heavens;
your faithfulness reaches to the skies.
Be exalted, O God, above the heavens,
and let your glory be over all the earth.

—*Psalm 108:1–5*

Week 23: Wednesday

We have different gifts, according to the grace given us. If a man's gift is prophesying, let him use it in proportion to his faith. If it is serving, let him serve; if it is teaching, let him teach; if it is encouraging, let him encourage; if it is contributing to the needs of others, let him give generously; if it is leadership, let him govern diligently; if it is showing mercy, let him do it cheerfully.

—*Romans 12:6–8*

If the ax is dull
and its edge unsharpened,
more strength is needed
but skill will bring success.

—*Ecclesiastes 10:10*

Yours, O LORD, is the greatness and the power
and the glory and the majesty and the splendor,
for everything in heaven and earth is yours.
Yours, O LORD, is the kingdom;
you are exalted as head over all.
Wealth and honor come from you;
you are the ruler of all things.
In your hands are strength and power
to exalt and give strength to all.

—*1 Chronicles 29:11–12*

Week 23: Thursday

You may say to yourself, "My power and the strength of my hands have produced this wealth for me." But remember the LORD your God, for it is he who gives you the ability to produce wealth, and so confirms his covenant, which he swore to your forefathers, as it is today.

—Deuteronomy 8:17–18

Now, our God, we give you thanks,
and praise your glorious name.

But who am I, and who are my people, that we should be able to give as generously as this? Everything comes from you, and we have given you only what comes from your hand.

—1 Chronicles 29:13–14

By the grace given me I say to every one of you: Do not think of yourself more highly than you ought, but rather think of yourself with sober judgment, in accordance with the measure of faith God has given you.

—Romans 12:3

Week 23: Friday

Every good and perfect gift is from above, coming down from the Father of the heavenly lights, who does not change like shifting shadows.

—James 1:17

"See, I have chosen Bezalel son of Uri, the son of Hur, of the tribe of Judah, and I have filled him with the Spirit of God, with skill, ability and knowledge in all kinds of crafts— to make artistic designs for work in gold, silver and bronze."

—Exodus 31:2–4

Then Moses summoned Bezalel and Oholiab and every skilled person to whom the LORD had given ability and who was willing to come and do the work.

—Exodus 36:2

Carefully follow the terms of this covenant, so that you may prosper in everything you do.

—Deuteronomy 29:9

"For the entrance to the tent make a curtain of blue, purple and scarlet yarn and finely twisted linen—the work of an embroiderer."

—Exodus 26:36

Week 23: Weekend

Each man has his own gift from God; one has this gift, another has that.

—*1 Corinthians 7:7*

Each one should use whatever gift he has received to serve others, faithfully administering God's grace in its various forms.

—*1 Peter 4:10*

Bless all his skills, O LORD,
and be pleased with the work of his hands.

—*Deuteronomy 33:11*

Moses said to the Lord, "O LORD, I have never been eloquent, neither in the past nor since you have spoken to your servant. I am slow of speech and tongue."
The LORD said to him, "Who gave man his mouth? Who makes him deaf or mute? Who gives him sight or makes him blind? Is it not I, the LORD? Now go; I will help you speak and will teach you what to say."

—*Exodus 4:10–12*

Week 24: Monday

Stop doing wrong,
learn to do right!
Seek justice,
encourage the oppressed.
Defend the cause of the fatherless,
plead the case of the widow.

"Come now, let us reason together,"
says the LORD.
"Though your sins are like scarlet,
they shall be as white as snow;
though they are red as crimson,
they shall be like wool.
If you are willing and obedient,
you will eat the best from the land."

—Isaiah 1:16–19

Week 24: Tuesday

"Fear the LORD and serve him with all faithfulness.
Throw away the gods your forefathers worshiped
beyond the River and in Egypt, and serve the LORD. But
if serving the LORD seems undesirable to you, then
choose for yourselves this day whom you will serve,
whether the gods your forefathers served beyond the
River, or the gods of the Amorites, in whose land you
are living. But as for me and my household, we will
serve the LORD."

—*Joshua 24:14–15*

Blessed are they who maintain justice,
who constantly do what is right.

—*Psalm 106:3*

How much better to get wisdom than gold,
to choose understanding rather than silver!

—*Proverbs 16:16*

Week 24: Wednesday

This day I call heaven and earth as witnesses against you that I have set before you life and death, blessings and curses. Now choose life, so that you and your children may live and that you may love the LORD your God, listen to his voice, and hold fast to him. For the LORD is your life, and he will give you many years in the land.

—Deuteronomy 30:19–20

Be very careful, then, how you live—not as unwise but as wise, making the most of every opportunity, because the days are evil.

—Ephesians 5:15–16

Now all has been heard;
*   here is the conclusion of the matter:*
Fear God and keep his commandments,
*   or this is the whole duty of man.*
For God will bring every deed into judgment,
*   including every hidden thing,*
*   whether it is good or evil.*

—Ecclesiastes 12:13–14

Week 24: Thursday

The LORD your God is testing you to find out whether you love him with all your heart and with all your soul. It is the Lord your God you must follow, and him you must revere. Keep his commands and obey him; serve him and hold fast to him.

—Deuteronomy 13:3–4

Since Christ suffered in his body, arm yourselves also with the same attitude, because he who has suffered in his body is done with sin. As a result, he does not live the rest of his earthly life for evil human desires, but rather for the will of God. For you have spent enough time in the past doing what pagans choose to do. . . . They think it strange that you do not plunge with them into the same flood of dissipation, and they heap abuse on you. But they will have to give account to him who is ready to judge the living and the dead. . . . The end of all things is near. Therefore be clear minded and self-controlled so that you can pray.

—1 Peter 4:1–5, 7

Week 24: Friday

Remember how the Lord your God led you all the way in the desert these forty years, to humble you and to test you in order to know what was in your heart, whether or not you would keep his commands.

—Deuteronomy 8:2

This is what the LORD says:

"Stand at the crossroads and look;
*   ask for the ancient paths,*
ask where the good way is, and walk in it,
*   and you will find rest for your souls."*

—Jeremiah 6:16

Lead me, O LORD, in your righteousness . . .
*   make straight your way before me.*

—Psalm 5:8

Week 24: Weekend

Blessed is the man
who does not walk in the counsel of the wicked
or stand in the way of sinners
or sit in the seat of mockers.
But his delight is in the law of the LORD,
and on his law he meditates day and night.

—Psalm 1:1–2

Teach me your way, O LORD;
lead me in a straight path.

—Psalm 27:11

Week 25: Monday

"Do not judge, or you too will be judged. For in the same way you judge others, you will be judged, and with the measure you use, it will be measured to you. "Why do you look at the speck of sawdust in your brother's eye and pay no attention to the plank in your own eye? How can you say to your brother, 'Let me take the speck out of your eye,' when all the time there is a plank in your own eye? You hypocrite, first take the plank out of your own eye, and then you will see clearly to remove the speck from your brother's eye."

—*Matthew 7:1–5*

May the Lord make your love increase and overflow for each other and for everyone else, just as ours does for you. May he strengthen your hearts so that you will be blameless and holy in the presence of our God and Father when our Lord Jesus comes with all his holy ones.

—*1 Thessalonians 3:12–13*

Week 25: Tuesday

Do not gloat when your enemy falls;
*   when he stumbles, do not let your*
*   heart rejoice,*
or the LORD will see and disapprove.

—Proverbs 24:17–18

"Speak the truth to each other, and render true and sound judgment in your courts; do not plot evil against your neighbor, and do not love to swear falsely. I hate all this," declares the LORD.

—Zechariah 8:14–17

Week 25: Wednesday

Blessed are the peacemakers,
for they will be called sons of God.

—Matthew 5:9

No one has ever seen God; but if we love one another, God lives in us and his love is made complete in us.

—1 John 4:12

Love is patient, love is kind. It does not envy, it does not boast, it is not proud. It is not rude, it is not self-seeking, it is not easily angered, it keeps no record of wrongs. Love does not delight in evil but rejoices with the truth. It always protects, always trusts, always hopes, always perseveres.
Love never fails.

—1 Corinthians 13:4–8

Week 25: Thursday

Jesus said,
"Love your enemies, do good to those who hate you,
bless those who curse you, pray for those who mistreat
you. If someone strikes you on one cheek, turn to him
the other also. If someone takes your cloak, do not stop
him from taking your tunic. Give to everyone who asks
you, and if anyone takes what belongs to you, do not
demand it back. Do to others as you would have them
do to you."

—Luke 6:27–31

Now that you have purified yourselves by obeying the
truth so that you have sincere love for your brothers,
love one another deeply, from the heart.

—1 Peter 1:22

Week 25: Friday

Jesus said,
"My command is this: Love each other as I have loved you. Greater love has no one than this, that he lay down his life for his friends. You are my friends if you do what I command. I no longer call you servants, because a servant does not know his master's business. Instead, I have called you friends, for everything that I learned from my Father I have made known to you. You did not choose me, but I chose you and appointed you to go and bear fruit—fruit that will last. Then the Father will give you whatever you ask in my name. This is my command: Love each other."

—John 15:12–17

Let us be self-controlled, putting on faith and love as a breastplate, and the hope of salvation as a helmet. For God did not appoint us to suffer wrath but to receive salvation through our Lord Jesus Christ. He died for us so that, whether we are awake or asleep, we may live together with him. Therefore encourage one another and build each other up, just as in fact you are doing.

—1 Thessalonians 5:8–11

Week 25: Weekend

Make every effort to add to your faith goodness; and to goodness, knowledge; and to knowledge, self-control; and to self-control, perseverance; and to perseverance, godliness; and to godliness, brotherly kindness; and to brotherly kindness, love.

—2 Peter 1:5–7

Brothers, do not slander one another. Anyone who speaks against his brother or judges him speaks against the law and judges it. When you judge the law, you are not keeping it, but sitting in judgment on it. There is only one Lawgiver and Judge, the one who is able to save and destroy. But you—who are you to judge your neighbor?

—James 4:11–12

Accept one another, then, just as Christ accepted you, in order to bring praise to God.

—Romans 15:7

Do not withhold good from those who deserve it,
when it is in your power to act.

—Proverbs 3:27

Week 26: Monday

Now faith is being sure of what we hope for and cer-
tain of what we do not see. This is what the ancients
were commended for. . . .
Without faith it is impossible to please God, because
anyone who comes to him must believe that he exists
and that he rewards those who earnestly seek him.

—Hebrews 11:1–2, 6

Though you have not seen Christ, you love him; and
even though you do not see him now, you believe in
him and are filled with an inexpressible and glorious
joy, for you are receiving the goal of your faith, the salvation of your souls.

—1 Peter 1:8–9

We live by faith, not by sight.

—2 Corinthians 5:7

Week 26: Tuesday

The LORD appeared to Abraham near the great trees of Mamre while he was sitting at the entrance to his tent in the heat of the day. Abraham looked up and saw three men standing nearby. When he saw them, he hurried from the entrance of his tent to meet them and bowed low to the ground. . . .

"Where is your wife Sarah?" they asked him.

"There, in the tent," he said.

Then the LORD said, "I will surely return to you about this time next year, and Sarah your wife will have a son."

Now Sarah was listening at the entrance to the tent, which was behind him. Abraham and Sarah were already old and well advanced in years, and Sarah was past the age of childbearing. So Sarah laughed to herself as she thought, "After I am worn out and my master is old, will I now have this pleasure?"

Then the LORD said to Abraham, "Why did Sarah laugh and say, 'Will I really have a child, now that I am old?' Is anything too hard for the LORD? I will return to you at the appointed time next year and Sarah will have a son."

Sarah was afraid, so she lied and said, "I did not laugh." But he said, "Yes, you did laugh."

—*Genesis 18:1–2, 9–15*

Week 26: Wednesday

Immediately Jesus made the disciples get into the boat and go on ahead of him to the other side, while he dismissed the crowd. After he had dismissed them, he went up on a mountainside by himself to pray. When evening came, he was there alone, but the boat was already a considerable distance from land, buffeted by the waves because the wind was against it.

During the fourth watch of the night Jesus went out to them, walking on the lake. When the disciples saw him walking on the lake, they were terrified. "It's a ghost," they said, and cried out in fear.

But Jesus immediately said to them: "Take courage! It is I. Don't be afraid."

"Lord, if it's you," Peter replied, "tell me to come to you on the water."

"Come," he said.

Then Peter got down out of the boat, walked on the water and came toward Jesus. But when he saw the wind, he was afraid and, beginning to sink, cried out, "Lord, save me!"

Immediately Jesus reached out his hand and caught him. "You of little faith," he said, "why did you doubt?" And when they climbed into the boat, the wind died down. Then those who were in the boat worshiped him, saying, "Truly you are the Son of God."

—*Matthew 14:22–33*

Week 26: Thursday

John's disciples told him about all these things [that Jesus was doing]. Calling two of them, he sent them to the Lord to ask, "Are you the one who was to come, or should we expect someone else?"

When the men came to Jesus, they said, "John the Baptist sent us to you to ask, 'Are you the one who was to come, or should we expect someone else?' "

At that very time Jesus cured many who had diseases, sicknesses and evil spirits, and gave sight to many who were blind. So he replied to the messengers, "Go back and report to John what you have seen and heard: The blind receive sight, the lame walk, those who have leprosy are cured, the deaf hear, the dead are raised, and the good news is preached to the poor. Blessed is the man who does not fall away on account of me."

—Luke 7:18–23

When You Have Doubts

Week 26: Friday

When Jesus, Peter, James and John came to the other disciples, they saw a large crowd around them and the teachers of the law arguing with them. As soon as all the people saw Jesus, they were overwhelmed with wonder and ran to greet him.

"What are you arguing with them about?" he asked.

A man in the crowd answered, "Teacher, I brought you my son, who is possessed by a spirit that has robbed him of speech. Whenever it seizes him, it throws him to the ground. He foams at the mouth, gnashes his teeth and becomes rigid. I asked your disciples to drive out the spirit, but they could not."

"O unbelieving generation," Jesus replied, "how long shall I stay with you? How long shall I put up with you? Bring the boy to me."

So they brought him. When the spirit saw Jesus, it immediately threw the boy into a convulsion. He fell to the ground and rolled around, foaming at the mouth. Jesus asked the boy's father, "How long has he been like this?"

"From childhood," he answered. "It has often thrown him into fire or water to kill him. But if you can do anything, take pity on us and help us."

" 'If you can'?" said Jesus. "Everything is possible for him who believes." Immediately the boy's father exclaimed, "I do believe; help me overcome my unbelief!"

—**Mark 9:14–24**

Week 26: Weekend

Now Thomas (called Didymus), one of the Twelve, was not with the disciples when Jesus came. So the other disciples told him, "We have seen the Lord!"
But he said to them, "Unless I see the nail marks in his hands and put my finger where the nails were, and put my hand into his side, I will not believe it."
A week later his disciples were in the house again, and Thomas was with them. Though the doors were locked, Jesus came and stood among them and said, "Peace be with you!" Then he said to Thomas, "Put your finger here; see my hands. Reach out your hand and put it into my side. Stop doubting and believe."
Thomas said to him, "My Lord and my God!"
Then Jesus told him, "Because you have seen me, you have believed; blessed are those who have not seen and yet have believed."
Jesus did many other miraculous signs in the presence of his disciples, which are not recorded in this book. But these are written that you may believe that Jesus is the Christ, the Son of God, and that by believing you may have life in his name.

—John 20:24–31

Week 27: Monday

Make it your ambition to lead a quiet life, to mind your own business and to work with your hands, just as we told you, so that your daily life may win the respect of outsiders and so that you will not be dependent on anybody.

—1 Thessalonians 4:11–12

Whatever you do, work at it with all your heart, as working for the Lord, not for men, since you know that you will receive an inheritance from the Lord as a reward. It is the Lord Christ you are serving.

—Colossians 3:23–24

The way of the sluggard is blocked with thorns,
but the path of the upright is a highway.

—Proverbs 15:19

Moreover, when God gives any man wealth and possessions, and enables him to enjoy them, to accept his lot and be happy in his work—this is a gift of God. He seldom reflects on the days of his life, because God keeps him occupied with gladness of heart.

—Ecclesiastes 5:19–20

Week 27: Tuesday

To this end I labor, struggling with all his energy, which so powerfully works in me. We proclaim him, admonishing and teaching everyone with all wisdom, so that we may present everyone perfect in Christ.

—*Colossians 1:28–29*

He who gathers crops in summer is a wise son,
but he who sleeps during harvest is a
disgraceful son.

—*Proverbs 10:5*

Be strong and courageous, and do the work. Do not be afraid or discouraged, for the Lᴏʀᴅ God, my God, is with you.

—*1 Chronicles 28:20*

Week 27: **Wednesday**

The plans of the diligent lead to profit
as surely as haste leads to poverty.

—*Proverbs 21:5*

He who loves pleasure will become poor;
whoever loves wine and oil will never be rich.

—*Proverbs 21:17*

Go to the ant, you sluggard;
consider its ways and be wise!
It has no commander,
no overseer or ruler,
yet it stores its provisions in summer
and gathers its food at harvest.

—*Proverbs 6:6–11*

Cast your cares on the LORD
and he will sustain you;
he will never let the righteous fall.

—*Psalm 55:22*

Week 27: Thursday

The sluggard buries his hand in the dish;
he will not even bring it back to his mouth!

—Proverbs 19:24

As for you, be strong and do not give up, for your work
will be rewarded.

—2 Chronicles 15:7

Nehemiah said,
[Those who opposed our project] were all trying to
frighten us, thinking, "Their hands will get too weak for
the work, and it will not be completed."
But I prayed, "Now strengthen my hands."

—Nehemiah 6:9

The Israelites had done all the work just as the LORD
had commanded Moses. Moses inspected the work
and saw that they had done it just as the LORD had
commanded. So Moses blessed them.

—Exodus 39:42–43

Week 27: Friday

Do not love sleep or you will grow poor;
stay awake and you will have food to spare.

—Proverbs 20:13

Do you see a man skilled in his work?
He will serve before kings;
he will not serve before obscure men.

—Proverbs 22:29

Do your best to present yourself to God as one
approved, a workman who does not need to be
ashamed and who correctly handles the word of truth.

—2 Timothy 2:15

He who works his land will have abundant food,
but he who chases fantasies lacks judgment.

—Proverbs 12:11

Week 27: **Weekend**

Do you not know that in a race all the runners run, but only one gets the prize? Run in such a way as to get the prize.

—1 Corinthians 9:24

May the favor of the Lord our God rest upon us;
    establish the work of our hands for us—
    yes, establish the work of our hands.

—Psalm 90:17

My heart took delight in all my work,
    and this was the reward for all my labor.

—Ecclesiastes 2:10

All hard work brings a profit,
    but mere talk leads only to poverty.

—Proverbs 14:23

Week 28: Monday

Jesus went through all the towns and villages, teaching in their synagogues, preaching the good news of the kingdom and healing every disease and sickness.

—Matthew 9:35

Jesus Christ is the same yesterday and today and forever.

—Hebrews 13:8

Is any one of you in trouble? He should pray. Is anyone happy? Let him sing songs of praise. Is any one of you sick? He should call the elders of the church to pray over him and anoint him with oil in the name of the Lord. And the prayer offered in faith will make the sick person well; the Lord will raise him up. If he has sinned, he will be forgiven. Therefore confess your sins to each other and pray for each other so that you may be healed. The prayer of a righteous man is powerful and effective.

—James 5:13–16

Week 28: Tuesday

A man's spirit sustains him in sickness.

—Proverbs 18:14

Praise the LORD, O my soul;
*   all my inmost being, praise his holy name.*
Praise the LORD, O my soul,
*   and forget not all his benefits—*
who forgives all your sins
*   and heals all your diseases,*
who redeems your life from the pit
*   and crowns you with love and compassion,*
who satisfies your desires with good things
*   so that your youth is renewed like the eagle's.*

—Psalm 103:1–5

Week 28: Wednesday

Do not be wise in your own eyes;
*   fear the LORD and shun evil.*
This will bring health to your body
*   and nourishment to your bones.*

—Proverbs 3:7–8

My son, pay attention to what I say;
*   listen closely to my words.*
Do not let them out of your sight,
*   keep them within your heart;*
for they are life to those who find them
*   and health to a man's whole body.*
Above all else, guard your heart,
*   for it is the wellspring of life.*

—Proverbs 4:20–23

The LORD heals the brokenhearted
*   and binds up their wounds.*

—Psalm 147:3

Week 28: Thursday

Heal me, O LORD, and I will be healed;
save me and I will be saved,
for you are the one I praise.

—*Jeremiah 17:14*

When Jesus came into Peter's house, he saw Peter's mother-in-law lying in bed with a fever. He touched her hand and the fever left her, and she got up and began to wait on him.
When evening came, many who were demon-possessed were brought to him, and he drove out the spirits with a word and healed all the sick. This was to fulfill what was spoken through the prophet Isaiah:

He took up our infirmities
and carried our diseases."

—*Matthew 8:14–17*

Week 28: Friday

When Jesus had entered Capernaum, a centurion came to him, asking for help. "Lord," he said, "my servant lies at home paralyzed and in terrible suffering."
Jesus said to him, "I will go and heal him."
The centurion replied, "Lord, I do not deserve to have you come under my roof. But just say the word, and my servant will be healed. For I myself am a man under authority, with soldiers under me. I tell this one, 'Go,' and he goes; and that one, 'Come,' and he comes. I say to my servant, 'Do this,' and he does it."
When Jesus heard this, he was astonished and said to those following him, "I tell you the truth, I have not found anyone in Israel with such great faith." . . .
Then Jesus said to the centurion, "Go! It will be done just as you believed it would." And his servant was healed at that very hour.

—*Matthew 8:5–10, 13*

Week 28: Weekend

A heart at peace gives life to the body.
—Proverbs 14:30

A cheerful look brings joy to the heart,
and good news gives health to the bones.

—Proverbs 15:30

A cheerful heart is good medicine,
but a crushed spirit dries up the bones.

—Proverbs 17:22

Pleasant words are a honeycomb,
sweet to the soul and healing to the bones.

—Proverbs 16:24

Week 29: Monday

Surely God is good to Israel,
*   to those who are pure in heart.*

But as for me, my feet had almost slipped;
*   I had nearly lost my foothold.*
For I envied the arrogant
*   when I saw the prosperity of the wicked. . . .*

This is what the wicked are like—
*   always carefree, they increase in wealth.*

Surely in vain have I kept my heart pure;
*   in vain have I washed my hands in innocence.*
All day long I have been plagued;
*   I have been punished every morning. . . .*

When I tried to understand all this,
*   it was oppressive to me*
till I entered the sanctuary of God;
*   then I understood their final destiny.*

—Psalm 73:1–3, 12–14, 16–17

Week 29: Tuesday

How can a young man keep his way pure?
  By living according to your word.
I seek you with all my heart;
  do not let me stray from your commands.
I have hidden your word in my heart
  that I might not sin against you.
Praise be to you, O LORD;
  teach me your decrees.
With my lips I recount
  all the laws that come from your mouth.
I rejoice in following your statutes
  as one rejoices in great riches.
I meditate on your precepts
  and consider your ways.
I delight in your decrees;
  I will not neglect your word.

—Psalm 119:9–16

Week 29: Wednesday

Do not conform any longer to the pattern of this world,
but be transformed by the renewing of your mind. Then
you will be able to test and approve what God's will
is—his good, pleasing and perfect will.

—Romans 12:2

"You have said, 'It is futile to serve God. What did we
gain by carrying out his requirements and going about
like mourners before the Lord Almighty? But now we
call the arrogant blessed. Certainly the evildoers prosper, and even those who challenge God escape.' "
Then those who feared the Lord talked with each other,
and the Lord listened and heard. A scroll of remem-
brance was written in his presence concerning those
who feared the Lord and honored his name.
"They will be mine," says the Lord Almighty, "in the day
when I make up my treasured possession. I will spare
them, just as in compassion a man spares his son who
serves him. And you will again see the distinction
between the righteous and the wicked, between those
who serve God and those who do not."

—Malachi 3:14–18

Week 29: Thursday

Prepare your minds for action; be self-controlled; set your hope fully on the grace to be given you when Jesus Christ is revealed. As obedient children, do not conform to the evil desires you had when you lived in ignorance. But just as he who called you is holy, so be holy in all you do; for it is written: "Be holy, because I am holy."

—1 Peter 1:13–16

Peter and the other apostles replied [to the authorities]: "We must obey God rather than men!

—Acts 5:29

The Israelites who had returned from the exile ate the Passover, together with all who had separated themselves from the unclean practices of their Gentile neighbors in order to seek the LORD, the God of Israel.

—Ezra 6:21

Week 29: Friday

"As for you, son of man, your countrymen are talking together about you by the walls and at the doors of the houses, saying to each other, 'Come and hear the message that has come from the LORD.' My people come to you, as they usually do, and sit before you to listen to your words, but they do not put them into practice. With their mouths they express devotion, but their hearts are greedy for unjust gain. Indeed, to them you are nothing more than one who sings love songs with a beautiful voice and plays an instrument well, for they hear your words but do not put them into practice. When all this comes true—and it surely will—then they will know that a prophet has been among them."

—Ezekiel 33:30–33

You are the children of the LORD your God. . . . You are a people holy to the LORD your God. Out of all the peoples on the face of the earth, the LORD has chosen you to be his treasured possession.

—Deuteronomy 14:1–2

Week 29: Weekend

O LORD, by your hand save me from wicked men,
from men of this world whose reward is in this life.

—Psalm 17:14

Join with others in following my example, brothers, and take note of those who live according to the pattern we gave you. For, as I have often told you before and now say again even with tears, many live as enemies of the cross of Christ. Their destiny is destruction, their god is their stomach, and their glory is in their shame. Their mind is on earthly things. But our citizenship is in heaven. And we eagerly await a Savior from there, the Lord Jesus Christ, who, by the power that enables him to bring everything under his control, will transform our lowly bodies so that they will be like his glorious body.

—Philippians 3:17–21

Week 30: Monday

As a prisoner for the Lord, then, I urge you to live a life worthy of the calling you have received. Be completely humble and gentle; be patient, bearing with one another in love. Make every effort to keep the unity of the Spirit through the bond of peace.

—Ephesians 4:1–3

Since an overseer is entrusted with God's work, he must be blameless—not overbearing, not quick-tempered, not given to drunkenness, not violent, not pursuing dishonest gain. Rather he must be hospitable, one who loves what is good, who is self-controlled, upright, holy and disciplined. He must hold firmly to the trustworthy message as it has been taught, so that he can encourage others by sound doctrine and refute those who oppose it.

—Titus 1:7–9

Week 30: Tuesday

A hot-tempered man must pay the penalty;
if you rescue him, you will have to do
it again.

—*Proverbs 19:19*

Better a patient man than a warrior,
a man who controls his temper
than one who takes a city.

—*Proverbs 16:32*

But the fruit of the Spirit is love, joy, peace, patience, kindness, goodness, faithfulness, gentleness and self-control. Against such things there is no law. Those who belong to Christ Jesus have crucified the sinful nature with its passions and desires. Since we live by the Spirit, let us keep in step with the Spirit. Let us not become conceited, provoking and envying each other.

—*Galatians 5:22–26*

Your beauty . . . should be that of your inner self, the unfading beauty of a gentle and quiet spirit, which is of great worth in God's sight.

—*1 Peter 3:3–4*

Week 30: Wednesday

Jonah was greatly displeased [at the LORD's compassion on his enemies] and became angry. He prayed to the LORD, . . . "I knew that you are a gracious and compassionate God, slow to anger and abounding in love, a God who relents from sending calamity. Now, O LORD, take away my life, for it is better for me to die than to live." But the LORD replied, "Have you any right to be angry?" Jonah went out and sat down at a place east of the city. There he made himself a shelter, sat in its shade and waited to see what would happen to the city of Nineveh. Then the LORD God provided a vine and made it grow up over Jonah to give shade for his head to ease his discomfort, and Jonah was very happy about the vine. But at dawn the next day God provided a worm, which chewed the vine so that it withered. When the sun rose, God provided a scorching east wind, and the sun blazed on Jonah's head so that he grew faint. He wanted to die, and said, "It would be better for me to die than to live." But God said to Jonah, "Do you have a right to be angry about the vine?" "I do," he said. "I am angry enough to die." But the LORD said, "You have been concerned about this vine, though you did not tend it or make it grow. It sprang up overnight and died overnight. But Nineveh has more than a hundred and twenty thousand people who cannot tell their right hand from their left. . . . Should I not be concerned about that great city?"

—*Jonah 4:1–11*

Week 30: Thursday

A patient man has great understanding,
but a quick-tempered man displays folly.

—Proverbs 14:29

Get rid of all bitterness, rage and anger, brawling and slander, along with every form of malice. Be kind and compassionate to one another, forgiving each other, just as in Christ God
forgave you.

—Ephesians 4:31–32

A fool shows his annoyance at once,
but a prudent man overlooks an insult.

—Proverbs 12:16

The heart of the righteous weighs its answers,
but the mouth of the wicked gushes evil.

—Proverbs 15:28

Week 30: Friday

Though you probe my heart and examine me at night,
though you test me, you will find nothing;
I have resolved that my mouth will not sin.
As for the deeds of men—
by the word of your lips
I have kept myself
from the ways of the violent.
My steps have held to your paths;
my feet have not slipped.

I call on you, O God, for you will answer me;
give ear to me and hear my prayer.
Show the wonder of your great love,
you who save by your right hand
those who take refuge in you from their foes.
Keep me as the apple of your eye;
hide me in the shadow of your wings
from the wicked who assail me,
from my mortal enemies who surround me.

—Psalm 17:3–9

Week 30: Weekend

*A hot-tempered man stirs up dissension,
    but a patient man calms a quarrel.*

—Proverbs 15:18

*A man of knowledge uses words with restraint,
    and a man of understanding is even-tempered.*

—Proverbs 17:27

*May the words of my mouth and the meditation of
my heart
    be pleasing in your sight,
    O LORD, my Rock and my Redeemer.*

—Psalm 19:14

*A wise man fears the LORD and shuns evil,
    but a fool is hotheaded and reckless.*

—Proverbs 14:16

Week 31: Monday

The LORD said to Moses, "Send some men to explore the land of Canaan, which I am giving to the Israelites. . . ." So at the LORD'S command Moses sent them out. . . . They went up and explored the land. . . . At the end of forty days they returned from exploring the land. . . . They gave Moses this account: "We went into the land to which you sent us, and . . . the people who live there are powerful, and the cities are fortified and very large. . . ." Then Caleb . . . said, "We should go up and take possession of the land, for we can certainly do it." But the men who had gone up with him said, "We can't attack those people; they are stronger than we are." And they spread among the Israelites a bad report about the land they had explored. . . . That night all the people of the community raised their voices and wept aloud. All the Israelites grumbled against Moses and Aaron, . . .the whole assembly talked about stoning them. . . .

[The LORD said to Moses,] . . . "Not one of them will ever see the land I promised on oath to their forefathers. No one who has treated me with contempt will ever see it. But because my servant Caleb has a different spirit and follows me wholeheartedly, I will bring him into the land he went to, and his descendants will inherit it."

—*Numbers 13:1–3, 21, 25, 27–28, 30–32; 14:1–2, 10, 23–24*

Week 31: Tuesday

Who can speak and have it happen
if the Lord has not decreed it?
Is it not from the mouth of the Most High
that both calamities and good things come?
Why should any living man complain
when punished for his sins?

Let us examine our ways and test them,
and let us return to the LORD.

—Lamentations 3:37–40

The fear of the LORD leads to life:
Then one rests content, untouched by
trouble.

—Proverbs 19:23

Godliness with contentment is great gain. For we brought nothing into the world, and we can take nothing out of it. But if we have food and clothing, we will be content with that.

—1 Timothy 6:6–8

Week 31: Wednesday

Lift your eyes and look to the heavens:
  Who created all these?
He who brings out the starry host one by one,
  and calls them each by name.
Because of his great power and mighty strength,
  not one of them is missing. . . .

Do you not know?
Have you not heard?
The LORD is the everlasting God,
  the Creator of the ends of the earth.
He will not grow tired or weary,
  and his understanding no one can fathom.

—Isaiah 40:24, 28

I have learned to be content whatever the circumstances. I know what it is to be in need, and I know what it is to have plenty. I have learned the secret of being content in any and every situation, whether well fed or hungry, whether living in plenty or in want. I can do everything through Christ who gives me strength.

—Philippians 4:11–13

Week 31: Thursday

You were taught, with regard to your former way of life, to put off your old self, which is being corrupted by its deceitful desires; to be made new in the attitude of your minds; and to put on the new self, created to be like God in true righteousness and holiness.

—Ephesians 4:22–24

Do everything without complaining or arguing, so that you may become blameless and pure, children of God without fault in a crooked and depraved generation, in which you shine like stars in the universe.

—Philippians 2:14–15

Devote yourselves to prayer, being watchful and thankful.

—Colossians 4:2

Week 31: Friday

As the deer pants for streams of water,
*   so my soul pants for you, O God.*
My soul thirsts for God, for the living God.
*   When can I go and meet with God?*
My tears have been my food
*   day and night,*
while men say to me all day long,
*   Where is your God?"*
These things I remember
*   as I pour out my soul:*
how I used to go with the multitude,
*   leading the procession to the house of God,*
with shouts of joy and thanksgiving
*   among the festive throng.*

Why are you downcast, O my soul?
*   Why so disturbed within me?*
Put your hope in God,
*   for I will yet praise him,*
*   my Savior and my God.*

—Psalm 42:1–6

Week 31: Weekend

I cry aloud to the LORD;
I lift up my voice to the LORD for mercy.
I pour out my complaint before him;
before him I tell my trouble.

When my spirit grows faint within me,
it is you who know my way. . . .

I cry to you, O LORD;
I say, "You are my refuge,
my portion in the land of the living."
Listen to my cry,
for I am in desperate need;
rescue me from those who pursue me,
for they are too strong for me.
Set me free from my prison,
that I may praise your name.

Then the righteous will gather about me
because of your goodness to me.

—Psalm 142:1–3, 5–7

Week 32: Monday

My dear brothers, take note of this: Everyone should be quick to listen, slow to speak and slow to become angry. Man's anger does not bring about the righteous life that God desires.

—Ephesians 4:19-20

A gentle answer turns away wrath,
but a harsh word stirs up anger.

—Proverbs 15:1

The end of a matter is better than its beginning,
and patience is better than pride.
Do not be quickly provoked in your spirit,
for anger resides in the lap of fools.

—Ecclesiastes 7:8–9

A fool gives full vent to his anger,
but a wise man keeps himself under control.

—Proverbs 29:11

Week 32: Tuesday

My dear brothers, take note of this: Everyone should be quick to listen, slow to speak and slow to become angry, for man's anger does not bring about the righteous life that God desires.

—James 1:19–20

Refrain from anger and turn from wrath;
do not fret—it leads only to evil.
For evil men will be cut off,
but those who hope in the LORD will inherit the
land.

—Psalm 37:8–9

Mockers stir up a city,
but wise men turn away anger.

—Proverbs 29:8

A kind man benefits himself,
but a cruel man brings trouble on himself.

—Proverbs 11:17

Week 32: Wednesday

As charcoal to embers and as wood to fire,
   so is a quarrelsome man for kindling strife.

—Proverbs 26:21

The LORD is compassionate and gracious,
   slow to anger, abounding in love.
He will not always accuse,
   nor will he harbor his anger forever;
he does not treat us as our sins deserve
   or repay us according to our iniquities.
For as high as the heavens are above the earth,
   so great is his love for those who fear him;
as far as the east is from the west,
   so far has he removed our transgressions from us.
As a father has compassion on his children,
   so the LORD has compassion on those who fear
   him.

—Psalm 103:8–13

Week 32: Thursday

When they hurled their insults at Jesus, he did not
retaliate; when he suffered, he made no threats.
Instead, he entrusted himself to God who judges justly.

—1 Peter 2:23

If you have played the fool and exalted yourself,
or if you have planned evil,
clap your hand over your mouth!
For as churning the milk produces butter,
and as twisting the nose produces blood,
so stirring up anger produces strife.

—Proverbs 30:32–33

"Do not seek revenge or bear a grudge against one of
your people, but love your neighbor as yourself. I am
the LORD.'"

—Leviticus 19:18

Week 32: Friday

We are fools for Christ. . . .
We work hard with our own hands. When we are
cursed, we bless; when we are persecuted, we endure
it, when we are slandered, we answer kindly.

—1 Corinthians 4:10, 12–13

Who is a God like you,
who pardons sin and forgives the transgression
of the remnant of his inheritance?
You do not stay angry forever
but delight to show mercy.
You will again have compassion on us;
you will tread our sins underfoot
and hurl all our iniquities into the depths of the
sea.

—Micah 7:18–19

Week 32: **Weekend**

Better a patient man than a warrior,
a man who controls his temper
than one who takes a city.

—Proverbs 16:32

Rend your heart
and not your garments.
Return to the LORD your God,
for he is gracious and compassionate,
slow to anger and abounding in love,
and he relents from sending calamity.

—Joel 2:13

Week 33: Monday

I went past the field of the sluggard,
*   past the vineyard of the man who lacks judgment;*
thorns had come up everywhere,
*   the ground was covered with weeds,*
*   and the stone wall was in ruins.*
I applied my heart to what I observed
*   and learned a lesson from what I saw:*
A little sleep, a little slumber,
*   a little folding of the hands to rest—*
and poverty will come on you like a bandit
*   and scarcity like an armed man.*

—Proverbs 24:30–34

Never be lacking in zeal, but keep your spiritual fervor, serving the Lord. Be joyful in hope, patient in affliction, faithful in prayer.

—Romans 12:11–12

Week 33: Tuesday

The sluggard says, "There is a lion in the road,
a fierce lion roaming the streets!"

As a door turns on its hinges,
so a sluggard turns on his bed.

The sluggard buries his hand in the dish;
he is too lazy to bring it back to his mouth.

The sluggard is wiser in his own eyes
than seven men who answer discreetly.

—Proverbs 26:13–16

We want each of you to show this same diligence to
the very end, in order to make your hope sure. We do
not want you to become lazy, but to imitate those who
through faith and patience inherit what has been
promised.

—Hebrews 6:11–12

Week 33: Wednesday

My dear brothers, stand firm. Let nothing move you.
Always give yourselves fully to the work of the Lord,
because you know that your labor in the Lord is not in
vain.

—1 Corinthians 15:58

Diligent hands will rule,
but laziness ends in slave labor.

—Proverbs 12:24

Laziness brings on deep sleep,
and the shiftless man goes hungry.

—Proverbs 19:15

Six days you shall labor, but on the seventh day you
shall rest; even during the plowing season and harvest
you must rest.

—Exodus 34:21

Week 33: Thursday

The sluggard craves and gets nothing,
but the desires of the diligent are fully satisfied.

—Proverbs 13:4

In the name of the Lord Jesus Christ, we command you, brothers, to keep away from every brother who is idle and does not live according to the teaching you received from
us. For you yourselves know how you ought to follow our example. We were not idle when we were with you, nor did we eat anyone's food without paying for it. On the contrary, we worked night and day, laboring and toiling so that we would not be a burden to any of you. We did this, not because we do not have the right to such help, but in order to make ourselves a model for you to follow. For even when we were with you, we gave you this rule: "If a man will not work, he shall not eat."
We hear that some among you are idle. They are not busy; they are busybodies. Such people we command and urge in the Lord Jesus Christ to settle down and earn the bread they eat. And as for you, brothers, never tire of doing what is right.

—2 Thessalonians 3:6–13

Week 33: Friday

These all look to you
    to give them their food at the proper time.
When you give it to them,
they gather it up;
    when you open your hand,
they are satisfied with good things.

—**Psalm 104:27–28**

Sow your seed in the morning,
    and at evening let not your hands be idle,
for you do not know which will succeed,
    whether this or that,
    or whether both will do equally well.

—**Ecclesiastes 11:6**

Week 33: Weekend

Lazy hands make a man poor,
but diligent hands bring wealth.

—Proverbs 10:4

The lazy man does not roast his game,
but the diligent prizes his possessions.

—Proverbs 12:27

If a man is lazy, the rafters sag;
if his hands are idle, the house leaks.

—Ecclesiastes 10:18

The sluggard's craving will be the death of him,
because his hands refuse to work.
All day long he craves for more,
but the righteous give without sparing.

—Proverbs 21:25–26

Week 34: Monday

Do nothing out of selfish ambition or vain conceit, but in humility consider others better than yourselves.

—Philippians 2:3

Remind the people to be subject to rulers and authorities, to be obedient, to be ready to do whatever is good, to slander no one, to be peaceable and considerate, and to show true humility toward all men.

—Titus 3:1–2

Live in harmony with one another. Do not be proud, but be willing to associate with people of low position. Do not be conceited.

—Romans 12:16

Week 34: Tuesday

To keep me from becoming conceited . . . there was given me a thorn in my flesh, a messenger of Satan, to torment me. Three times I pleaded with the Lord to take it away from me. But he said to me, "My grace is sufficient for you, for my power is made perfect in weakness." Therefore I will boast all the more gladly about my weaknesses, so that Christ's power may rest on me. That is why, for Christ's sake, I delight in weaknesses, in insults, in hardships, in persecutions, in difficulties. For when I am weak, then I am strong.

—2 Corinthians 12:7–10

Jesus said, "I praise you, Father, Lord of heaven and earth, because you have hidden [your mysteries] from the wise and learned, and revealed them to little children. Yes, Father, for this was your good pleasure."

—Matthew 11:25–26

*The LORD mocks proud mockers
        but gives grace to the humble.*

—Proverbs 3:34

Week 34: Wednesday

Who is wise and understanding among you? Let him show it by his good life, by deeds done in the humility that comes from wisdom.

—James 3:13

Jesus said, "Therefore, whoever humbles himself like this child is the greatest in the kingdom of heaven."

—Matthew 18:4

*When pride comes, then comes disgrace,
    but with humility comes wisdom.*

—Proverbs 11:2

*Pride goes before destruction,
    a haughty spirit before a fall.
Better to be lowly in spirit and among the oppressed
    than to share plunder with the proud.
Whoever gives heed to instruction prospers,
    and blessed is he who trusts in the LORD.*

—Proverbs 16:18–20

Week 34: Thursday

All of you, clothe yourselves with humility toward one another, because,

"God opposes the proud
but gives grace to the humble."

Humble yourselves, therefore, under God's mighty hand, that he may lift you up in due time.

—1 Peter 5:5–6

Love the Lord, all his saints!
The Lord preserves the faithful,
but the proud he pays back in full.
Be strong and take heart,
all you who hope in the Lord.

—Psalm 31:23–24

You, O Lord, save the humble
but bring low those whose eyes are haughty.

—Psalm 18:27

Week 34: Friday

He got up from the meal, took off his outer clothing, and wrapped a towel around his waist. After that, he poured water into a basin and began to wash his disciples' feet, drying them with the towel that was wrapped around him.

When he had finished washing their feet, he put on his clothes and returned to his place. "Do you understand what I have done for you?" he asked them.

"You call me 'Teacher' and 'Lord,' and rightly so, for that is what I am. Now that I, your Lord and Teacher, have washed your feet, you also should wash one another's feet.

I have set you an example that you should do as I have done for you. I tell you the truth, no servant is greater than his
master, nor is a messenger greater than the one who sent him.

—*John 13:4–5, 12–16*

Week 34: Weekend

"Let not the wise man boast of his wisdom
or the strong man boast of his strength
or the rich man boast of his riches,
but let him who boasts boast about this:
that he understands and knows me,
that I am the LORD, who exercises kindness,
justice and righteousness on earth,
for in these I delight,"
declares the LORD.

—Jeremiah 9:23–24

We do not dare to classify or compare ourselves with some who commend themselves. When they measure themselves by themselves and compare themselves with themselves, they are not wise. … But, "Let him who boasts boast in the Lord."

—2 Corinthians 10:12, 17

Now I, Nebuchadnezzar, praise and exalt and glorify the King of heaven, because everything he does is right and all his ways are just. And those who walk in pride he is able to humble.

—Daniel 4:37

Week 35: Monday

I will be glad and rejoice in your love,
for you saw my affliction
and knew the anguish of my soul.
You have not handed me over to the enemy
but have set my feet in a spacious place.

Be merciful to me, O LORD, for I am in distress;
my eyes grow weak with sorrow,
my soul and my body with grief.
My life is consumed by anguish
and my years by groaning;
my strength fails because of my affliction,
and my bones grow weak. . . .
I trust in you, O LORD.
I say, "You are my God."
My times are in your hands;
deliver me from my enemies
and from those who pursue me.
Let your face shine on your servant;
save me in your unfailing love.

—Psalm 31:7-10, 14-16

Week 35: Tuesday

Wait for the LORD.
  be strong and take heart
and wait for the LORD.

—Psalm 27:14

When you pass through the waters,
I will be with you;
  and when you pass through the rivers,
  they will not sweep over you.
When you walk through the fire,
  you will not be burned;
  the flames will not set you ablaze.
For I am the LORD, your God,
  the Holy One of Israel, your Savior.

—Isaiah 43:2–3

Week 35: **Wednesday**

In you, O LORD, I have taken refuge;
let me never be put to shame;
deliver me in your righteousness.
Turn your ear to me,
come quickly to my rescue;
be my rock of refuge,
a strong fortress to save me.
Since you are my rock and my fortress,
for the sake of your name lead and guide me.
Free me from the trap that is set for me,
for you are my refuge.
Into your hands I commit my spirit;
redeem me, O LORD, the God of truth.

—Psalm 31:1–5

My flesh and my heart may fail,
but God is the strength of my heart
and my portion forever.

—Psalm 73:26

Week 35: Thursday

How great is your goodness,
     which you have stored up for those who fear you,
which you bestow in the sight of men
     on those who take refuge in you.
In the shelter of your presence you hide them
     from the intrigues of men;
in your dwelling you keep them safe
     from accusing tongues.

Praise be to the LORD,
     for he showed his wonderful love to me
     when I was in a besieged city.
In my alarm I said,
     "I am cut off from your sight!"
Yet you heard my cry for mercy
     when I called to you for help.

—Psalm 31:19–22

Week 35: Friday

Do not fear, for I am with you;
do not be dismayed, for I am your God.
I will strengthen you and help you;
I will uphold you with my righteous right hand.

All who rage against you
will surely be ashamed and disgraced;
those who oppose you
will be as nothing and perish.
Though you search for your enemies,
you will not find them.
Those who wage war against you
will be as nothing at all.
For I am the LORD, your God,
who takes hold of your right hand
and says to you, Do not fear;
I will help you.

—Isaiah 41:10–13

Week 35: Weekend

The Sovereign LORD has given me an instructed tongue,
  to know the word that sustains the weary.
He wakens me morning by morning,
  wakens my ear to listen like one being taught.
The Sovereign LORD has opened my ears,
  and I have not been rebellious;
  I have not drawn back. . . .

Because the Sovereign LORD helps me,
  I will not be disgraced.
Therefore have I set my face like flint,
  and I know I will not be put to shame.
He who vindicates me is near.
  Who then will bring charges against me?
  Let us face each other!
Who is my accuser?
  Let him confront me!
It is the Sovereign LORD who helps me.
  Who is he that will condemn me?

—Isaiah 50:4–5, 7–9

Week 36: Monday

Now then, my sons, listen to me;
do not turn aside from what I say.
Keep to a path far from her,
do not go near the door of her house,
lest you give your best strength to others
and your years to one who is cruel,
lest strangers feast on your wealth
and your toil enrich another man's house.
At the end of your life you will groan,
when your flesh and body are spent.
You will say, "How I hated discipline!
How my heart spurned correction!
I would not obey my teachers
or listen to my instructors.
I have come to the brink of utter ruin
in the midst of the whole assembly."

—Proverbs 5:7–14

Week 36: Tuesday

He who ignores discipline comes to poverty and shame,
>   *but whoever heeds correction is honored.*

—Proverbs 13:18

He who obeys instructions guards his life.

—Proverbs 19:16

Listen to advice and accept instruction,
>   *and in the end you will be wise.*

—Proverbs 19:20

Week 36: Wednesday

The way of a fool seems right to him,
but a wise man listens to advice.

—Proverbs 12:15

Stern discipline awaits him who leaves the path;
he who hates correction will die.

A mocker resents correction;
he will not consult the wise.

—Proverbs 15:10–12

For lack of guidance a nation falls,
but many advisers make victory sure.

—Proverbs 11:14

Week 36: Thursday

He who listens to a life-giving rebuke
will be at home among the wise.

—Proverbs 15:31

Wounds from a friend can be trusted,
but an enemy multiplies kisses.

—Proverbs 27:6

Perfume and incense bring joy to the heart,
and the pleasantness of one's friend springs from
his earnest counsel.

—Proverbs 27:9

As iron sharpens iron,
so one man sharpens another.

—Proverbs 27:17

Week 36: Friday

A wise son heeds his father's instruction,
but a mocker does not listen to rebuke.

—Proverbs 13:1

Pride only breeds quarrels,
but wisdom is found in those who take advice.

—Proverbs 13:10

A fool spurns his father's discipline,
but whoever heeds correction shows prudence.

—Proverbs 15:5

He who scorns instruction will pay for it,
but he who respects a command is rewarded.

—Proverbs 13:13

Week 36: Weekend

Rebuke a wise man and he will love you.
Instruct a wise man and he will be wiser still;
teach a righteous man and he will add to his
learning.

—Proverbs 9:8–9

He who rebukes a man will in the end gain more favor
than he who has a flattering tongue.

—Proverbs 28:23

Make plans by seeking advice;
if you wage war, obtain guidance.

—Proverbs 20:18

Week 37: Monday

Wisdom is found on the lips of the discerning.

—Proverbs 10:13

Test everything. Hold on to the good. Avoid every kind of evil. May God himself, the God of peace, sanctify you through and through. May your whole spirit, soul and body be kept blameless at the coming of our Lord Jesus Christ. The one who calls you is faithful and he will do it.

—1 Thessalonians 5:21–24

For the ear tests words
    as the tongue tastes food.
Let us discern for ourselves what is right;
    let us learn together what is good.

—Job 34:3–4

Week 37: Tuesday

Jesus said, "When he, the Spirit of truth, comes, he will guide you into all truth. He will not speak on his own; he will speak only what he hears, and he will tell you what is yet to come."

—John 16:13

Reflect on what I am saying, for the Lord will give you insight into all this.

—2 Timothy 2:7

The wise in heart are called discerning,
and pleasant words promote instruction.

—Proverbs 16:21

Week 37: Wednesday

*A rebuke impresses a man of discernment
more than a hundred lashes a fool.*

—Proverbs 17:10

*The discerning heart seeks knowledge,
but the mouth of a fool feeds on folly.*

—Proverbs 15:14

We are from God, and whoever knows God listens to
us; but whoever is not from God does not listen to us.
This is how we recognize the Spirit of truth and the
spirit of falsehood.

—1 John 4:6

*A simple man believes anything,
but a prudent man gives thought to his steps.*

—Proverbs 14:15

Week 37: Thursday

Be as shrewd as snakes and as innocent as doves.
Be on your guard.

—Matthew 10:16–17

*Who is wise? He will realize these things.
      Who is discerning? He will understand them.
The ways of the LORD are right;
      the righteous walk in them,
      but the rebellious stumble in them.*

—Hosea 14:9

*The mocker seeks wisdom and finds none,
      but knowledge comes easily to the discerning.*

—Proverbs 14:6

*My son, preserve sound judgment and discernment,
      do not let them out of your sight.*

—Proverbs 3:21

Week 37: Friday

A prudent man sees danger and takes refuge,
    but the simple keep going and suffer for it.

—Proverbs 22:3

The LORD guards the course of the just
    and protects the way of his faithful ones.
Then you will understand what is right and just
    and fair—every good path.
For wisdom will enter your heart,
    and knowledge will be pleasant to your soul.
Discretion will protect you,
    and understanding will guard you.

—Proverbs 2:8–11

Wisdom reposes in the heart of the discerning.

—Proverbs 14:33

Week 37: Weekend

At Gibeon the LORD appeared to Solomon during the night in a dream, and God said, "Ask for whatever you want me to give you." Solomon answered, "You have shown great kindness to your servant, my father David, because he was faithful to you and righteous and upright in heart. You have continued this great kindness to him and have given him a son to sit on his throne this very day. "Now, O LORD my God, you have made your servant king in place of my father David. But I am only a little child and do not know how to carry out my duties. Your servant is here among the people you have chosen, a great people, too numerous to count or number. So give your servant a discerning heart to govern your people and to distinguish between right and wrong. For who is able to govern this great people of yours?" The Lord was pleased that Solomon had asked for this. So God said to him, "Since you have asked … for discernment in administering justice, I will do what you have asked. I will give you a wise and discerning heart, so that there will never have been anyone like you, nor will there ever be. Moreover, I will give you what you have not asked for—both riches and honor—so that in your lifetime you will have no equal among kings. And if you walk in my ways and obey my statutes and commands as David your father did, I will give you a long life."

— *1 Kings 3:5–14*

Week 38: Monday

Therefore each of you must put off falsehood and speak truthfully to his neighbor, for we are all members of one body.

—*Ephesians 4:25*

The righteous hate what is false,
but the wicked bring shame and disgrace.

—*Proverbs 13:5*

A fortune made by a lying tongue
is a fleeting vapor and a deadly snare.

—*Proverbs 21:6*

I will maintain my righteousness and never let go of it;
my conscience will not reproach me as long as
I live.

—*Job 27:6*

Week 38: Tuesday

Therefore, rid yourselves of all malice and all deceit, hypocrisy, envy, and slander of every kind. Like new-born babies, crave pure spiritual milk, so that by it you may grow up in your salvation.

—1 Peter 2:1–2

God is not a man, that he should lie,
nor a son of man, that he should change his mind.
Does he speak and then not act?
Does he promise and not fulfill?

—Numbers 23:19

The heart is deceitful above all things
and beyond cure.
Who can understand it?

"I the LORD search the heart
and examine the mind,
to reward a man according to his conduct,
according to what his deeds deserve."

—Jeremiah 17:9–10

Week 38: Wednesday

An honest answer
is like a kiss on the lips.

—Proverbs 24:26

"Go up and down the streets of Jerusalem,
look around and consider,
search through her squares.
If you can find but one person
who deals honestly and seeks the truth,
I will forgive this city.
Although they say, 'As surely as the LORD lives,'
still they are swearing falsely."

O LORD, do not your eyes look for truth?

—Jeremiah 5:1–3

He whose walk is blameless
and who does what is righteous,
who speaks the truth from his heart
who lends his money without usury
and does not accept a bribe against the innocent.

He who does these things
will never be shaken.

—Psalm 15:2, 5

Week 38: Thursday

*He who walks righteously
    and speaks what is right,*

*who rejects gain from extortion
    and keeps his hand from accepting bribes,*

*who stops his ears against plots of murder
    and shuts his eyes against contemplating evil—*

*this is the man who will dwell on the heights,
    whose refuge will be the mountain fortress.*

*His bread will be supplied,
    and water will not fail him.*

—Isaiah 33:15–16

You must have accurate and honest weights and measures, so that you may live long in the land the LORD your God is giving you.

—Deuteronomy 25:15

Week 38: Friday

I will sing of your love and justice;
to you, O LORD, I will sing praise.
I will be careful to lead a blameless life—
when will you come to me?

I will walk in my house
with blameless heart.
I will set before my eyes
no vile thing.

The deeds of faithless men I hate;
they will not cling to me.
Men of perverse heart shall be far from me;
I will have nothing to do with evil.

Whoever slanders his neighbor in secret,
him will I put to silence;
whoever has haughty eyes and a proud heart,
him will I not endure.

My eyes will be on the faithful in the land,
that they may dwell with me;
he whose walk is blameless
will minister to me.

—Psalm 101:1–6

Week 38: Weekend

Help, LORD, for the godly are no more;
    the faithful have vanished from among men.
Everyone lies to his neighbor;
    their flattering lips speak with deception.

May the LORD cut off all flattering lips
    and every boastful tongue
that says, "We will triumph with our tongues;
    we own our lips—who is our master?"

"Because of the oppression of the weak
    and the groaning of the needy,
I will now arise," says the LORD.
    "I will protect them from those who malign them."
And the words of the LORD are flawless,
    like silver refined in a furnace of clay,
    purified seven times.

O LORD, you will keep us safe
    and protect us from such people forever.

—Psalm 12:1–8

Week 39: Monday

One thing I ask of the LORD,
this is what I seek:
that I may dwell in the house of the LORD
all the days of my life,
to gaze upon the beauty of the LORD
and to seek him in his temple.
For in the day of trouble
he will keep me safe in his dwelling;
he will hide me in the shelter of his tabernacle
and set me high upon a rock.
Then my head will be exalted
above the enemies who surround me;
at his tabernacle will I sacrifice with shouts of joy;
I will sing and make music to the LORD.

—Psalm 27:4–6

Week 39: **Tuesday**

The word of the LORD came to [Jeremiah], saying,

*"Before I formed you in the womb I knew you,
    before you were born I set you apart;
    I appointed you as a prophet to the nations."*

"Ah, sovereign LORD," [he] said, "I do not know how
to speak; I am only a child."
But the LORD said [to him,] "Do not say, 'I am only
a child.' "
You must go to everyone I send you to and say whatever I command you. Do not be afraid of them, for I am
with you and will rescue you," declares the LORD.

—*Jeremiah 1:4–8*

*The LORD is with me; I will not be afraid.
    What can man do to me?
The LORD is with me; he is my helper.
    I will look in triumph on my enemies.*

—*Psalm 118:6–7*

Week 39: Wednesday

Surely God is my salvation;
I will trust and not be afraid.
The LORD, the LORD, is my strength and my song;
he has become my salvation.

—*Isaiah 12:2*

God did not give us a spirit of timidity, but a spirit of power, of love and of self-discipline.

—*2 Timothy 1:7*

When I am afraid,
I will trust in you.
In God, whose word I praise,
in God I trust; I will not be afraid.
What can mortal man do to me?

—*Psalm 56:3–4*

Week 39: Thursday

God has said,

"Never will I leave you;
never will I forsake you."

So we say with confidence,

"The Lord is my helper; I will not be afraid.
What can man do to me?"

—Hebrews 13:5–6

He who dwells in the shelter of the Most High
will rest in the shadow of the Almighty.
I will say of the LORD, "He is my refuge and my fortress,
my God, in whom I trust."

—Psalm 91:1–2

Week 39: Friday

"Then Moses summoned Joshua and said to him in the presence of all Israel, "Be strong and courageous, for you must go with this people into the land that the LORD swore to their forefathers to give them, and you must divide it among them as their inheritance. The LORD himself goes before you and will be with you; he will never leave you nor forsake you. Do not be afraid; do not be discouraged."

—*Deuteronomy 31:7-8*

Those who are led by the Spirit of God are sons of God. For you did not receive a spirit that makes you a slave again to fear, but you received the Spirit of sonship. And by him we cry, "*Abba*, Father." The Spirit himself testifies with our spirit that we are God's children. Now if we are children, then we are heirs—heirs of God and coheirs with Christ, if indeed we share in his sufferings in order that we may also share in his glory.

—*Romans 8:14–17*

Week 39: **Weekend**

Jesus said,
"Peace I leave with you; my peace I give you. I do not
give to you as the world gives. Do not let your hearts
be troubled and do not be afraid."

—John 14:27

*My enemies will turn back
    when I call for help.
    By this I will know that God is for me.
In God, whose word I praise,
    in the LORD, whose word I praise—
in God I trust; I will not be afraid.
    What can man do to me?*

—Psalm 56:9–11

God is love. Whoever lives in love lives in God, and God
in him. In this way, love is made complete among us so
that we will have confidence on the day of judgment,
because in this world we are like him. There is no fear
in love. But perfect love drives out fear.

—1 John 4:16–18

Week 40: Monday

I am not writing you a new command but one we have had from the beginning. I ask that we love one another. And this is love: that we walk in obedience to his commands. As you have heard from the beginning, his command is that you walk in love.

—2 John 5–6

We who are strong ought to bear with the failings of the weak and not to please ourselves. Each of us should please his neighbor for his good, to build him up. For even Christ did not please himself but, as it is written: "The insults of those who insult you have fallen on me." For everything that was written in the past was written to teach us, so that through endurance and the encouragement of the Scriptures we might have hope.

—Romans 15:1–4

Many a man claims to have unfailing love,
but a faithful man who can find?

—Proverbs 20:6

Week 40: Tuesday

In Christ Jesus . . . the only thing that counts is faith expressing itself through love.

—Galatians 5:6

This is how we know what love is: Jesus Christ laid down his life for us. And we ought to lay down our lives for our brothers.

—1 John 3:16

Be imitators of God, as dearly loved children, and live a life of love, just as Christ loved us and gave himself up for us.

—Ephesians 5:1–2

We love because God first loved us. If anyone says, "I love God," yet hates his brother, he is a liar. For anyone who does not love his brother, whom he has seen, cannot love God, whom he has not seen. And he has given us this command: Whoever loves God must also love his brother.

—1 John 4:19–21

Week 40: Wednesday

Blessed are the merciful,
for they will be shown mercy.

—*Matthew 5:7*

Praise be to the God and Father of our Lord Jesus Christ, the Father of compassion and the God of all comfort, who comforts us in all our troubles, so that we can comfort those in any trouble with the comfort we ourselves have received from God.

—*2 Corinthians 1:3–4*

As believers in our glorious Lord Jesus Christ, don't show favoritism. . . . If you really keep the royal law found in Scripture, "Love your neighbor as yourself," you are doing right.

—*James 2:1, 8*

Week 40: Thursday

Love must be sincere. Hate what is evil; cling to what is good. Be devoted to one another in brotherly love. Honor one another above yourselves. . . . Share with God's people who are in need. Practice hospitality. Bless those who persecute you; bless and do not curse. Rejoice with those who rejoice; mourn with those who mourn. Live in harmony with one another.

—Romans 12:9–10, 13–16

Like one who takes away a garment on a cold day,
or like vinegar poured on soda,
is one who sings songs to a heavy heart.

—Proverbs 25:20

The purposes of a man's heart are deep waters,
but a man of understanding draws them out.

—Proverbs 20:5

Week 40: Friday

Live in peace with each other. And we urge you, brothers, warn those who are idle, encourage the timid, help the weak, be patient with everyone. Make sure that nobody pays back wrong for wrong, but always try to be kind to each other and to everyone else.

—*1 Thessalonians 5:13–15*

Dear children, let us not love with words or tongue but with actions and in truth.

—*1 John 3:18*

Hearing that Jesus had silenced the Sadducees, the Pharisees got together. One of them, an expert in the law, tested him with this question:
"Teacher, which is the greatest commandment in the Law?" Jesus replied: " 'Love the Lord your God with all your heart and with all your soul and with all your mind.' This is the first and greatest commandment. And the second is like it: 'Love your neighbor as yourself.' All the Law and the Prophets hang on these two commandments."

—*Matthew 22:34–40*

Week 40: Weekend

Not many of you should presume to be teachers, my brothers, because you know that we who teach will be judged more strictly. We all stumble in many ways. If anyone is never at fault in what he says, he is a perfect man, able to keep his whole body in check.

—James 3:1–2

Do nothing out of selfish ambition or vain conceit, but in humility consider others better than yourselves. Each of you should look not only to your own interests, but also to the interests of others.

—Philippians 2:3–4

Carry each other's burdens, and in this way you will fulfill the law of Christ.

—Galatians 6:2

As for me, far be it from me that I should sin against the LORD by failing to pray for you. And I will teach you the way that is good and right. But be sure to fear the LORD and serve him faithfully with all your heart; consider what great things he has done for you.

—1 Samuel 12:23–24

Week 41: Monday

My dear brothers, take note of this: Everyone should be quick to listen, slow to speak and slow to become angry.

—James 1:19

Jesus said,
"Therefore consider carefully how you listen. Whoever has will be given more; whoever does not have, even what he thinks he has will be taken from him."

—Luke 8:18

The LORD said to Jeremiah, "Proclaim all these words in the towns of Judah and in the streets of Jerusalem: 'Listen to the terms of this covenant and follow them. From the time I brought your forefathers up from Egypt until today, I warned them again and again, saying, "Obey me." But they did not listen or pay attention; instead, they followed the stubbornness of their evil hearts. So I brought on them all the curses of the covenant I had commanded them to follow but that they did not keep.' "

—Jeremiah 11:6–8

Week 41: Tuesday

He who answers before listening—
that is his folly and his shame.

—Proverbs 18:13

Do not merely listen to the word, and so deceive your-
selves. Do what it says. Anyone who listens to the
word but does not do what it says is like a man who
looks at his face in a mirror and, after looking at him-
self, goes away and immediately forgets what he looks
like. But the man who looks intently into the perfect
law that gives freedom, and continues to do this, not
forgetting what he has heard, but doing it—he will be
blessed in what he does.

—James 1:22–25

He who guards his lips guards his life,
but he who speaks rashly will come to ruin.

—Proverbs 13:3

Week 41: Wednesday

When words are many, sin is not absent,
but he who holds his tongue is wise.

—Proverbs 10:19

All kinds of animals, birds, reptiles and creatures of the sea are being tamed and have been tamed by man, but no man can tame the tongue. It is a restless evil, full of deadly poison.
With the tongue we praise our Lord and Father, and with it we curse men, who have been made in God's likeness. Out of the same mouth come praise and cursing. My brothers, this should not be.

—James 3:7–10

The wise in heart accept commands,
but a chattering fool comes to ruin.

—Proverbs 10:8

Week 41: Thursday

At Marah the LORD made a decree and a law for the Israelites, and there he tested them. He said, "If you listen carefully to the voice of the LORD your God and do what is right in his eyes, if you pay attention to his commands and keep all his decrees, I will not bring on you any of the diseases I brought on the Egyptians, for I am the LORD, who heals you."

—Exodus 15:25–26

Apply your heart to instruction
and your ears to words of knowledge.

—Proverbs 23:12

Jeremiah said of the Israelites:
To whom can I speak and give warning?
Who will listen to me?
Their ears are closed
so they cannot hear.
The word of the LORD is offensive to them;
they find no pleasure in it.

—Jeremiah 6:10

Week 41: Friday

Do you see a man who speaks in haste?
There is more hope for a fool than for him.

—Proverbs 29:20

Then Job replied to the LORD:

"I know that you can do all things;
no plan of yours can be thwarted.
You asked, 'Who is this that obscures my counsel
without knowledge?'
Surely I spoke of things I did not understand,
things too wonderful for me to know.

"You said, 'Listen now, and I will speak;
I will question you,
and you shall answer me.'
My ears had heard of you
but now my eyes have seen you."

—Job 42:1–5

Week 41: Weekend

*Even a fool is thought wise if he keeps silent,
and discerning if he holds his tongue.*

—Proverbs 17:28

So Eli told Samuel, "Go and lie down, and if he calls
you, say, 'Speak, LORD, for your servant is listening.' "
So Samuel went and lay down in his place.

—1 Samuel 3:9

*Set a guard over my mouth, O LORD;
keep watch over the door of my lips.*

—Psalm 141:3

Week 42: Monday

Good understanding wins favor,
but the way of the unfaithful is hard.

—Proverbs 13:15

Gold there is, and rubies in abundance,
but lips that speak knowledge are a rare jewel.

—Proverbs 20:15

Even a child is known by his actions,
by whether his conduct is pure and right.

—Proverbs 20:11

Week 42: Tuesday

The memory of the righteous will be a blessing.

—Proverbs 10:7

Jesus said,
"You are the light of the world. A city on a hill cannot be hidden. Neither do people light a lamp and put it under a bowl. Instead they put it on its stand, and it gives light to everyone in the house. In the same way, let your light shine before men, that they may see your good deeds and praise your Father in heaven."

—Matthew 5:14–16

You are a people holy to the Lord your God. The Lord your God has chosen you out of all the peoples on the face of the earth to be his people, his treasured possession.

—Deuteronomy 7:6

A kindhearted woman gains respect. . . .
A kind man benefits himself.

—Proverbs 11:16–17

Week 42: Wednesday

Do not exalt yourself in the king's presence,
and do not claim a place among great men;
it is better for him to say to you, "Come up here,"
than for him to humiliate you before a nobleman.

—Proverbs 25:6–7

My son, do not forget my teaching,
but keep my commands in your heart,
for they will prolong your life many years
and bring you prosperity.

Let love and faithfulness never leave you;
bind them around your neck,
write them on the tablet of your heart.
Then you will win favor and a good name
in the sight of God and man.

—Proverbs 3:1–4

Week 42: Thursday

A man is praised according to his wisdom.

—Proverbs 12:8

A dispute arose among Jesus' disciples as to which of them was considered to be the greatest. Jesus said to them, "The kings of the Gentiles lord it over them; and those who exercise authority over them call themselves Benefactors. But you are not to be like that. Instead the greatest among you should be like the youngest, and the one who rules like the one who serves. For who is greater, the one who is at the table or the one who serves? Is it not the one who is at the table? But I am among you as one who serves."

—Luke 22:24–27

Jesus said,
"Whoever welcomes this little child in my name welcomes me; and whoever welcomes me welcomes the one who sent me. For he who is least among you all—he is the greatest."

—Luke 9:48

Week 42: Friday

A wife of noble character who can find?
She is worth far more than rubies.
Her husband has full confidence in her
and lacks nothing of value.
She brings him good, not harm,
all the days of her life. . . .

Her husband is respected at the city gate,
where he takes his seat among the elders
of the land. . . .

She is clothed with strength and dignity;
she can laugh at the days to come.
She speaks with wisdom,
and faithful instruction is on her tongue. . . .

Her children arise and call her blessed;
her husband also, and he praises her:
"Many women do noble things,
but you surpass them all."
Charm is deceptive, and beauty is fleeting;
but a woman who fears the LORD is to be praised.
Give her the reward she has earned,
and let her works bring her praise at the city gate.

—Proverbs 31:10–12, 23, 25–26, 28–31

Week 42: Weekend

The administrators and the satraps tried to find
grounds for charges against Daniel in his conduct of
government affairs, but they were unable to do so.
They could find no corruption in him, because he was
trustworthy and neither corrupt nor negligent.

—*Daniel 6:4*

A good name is more desirable than great riches;
to be esteemed is better than silver or gold.

—*Proverbs 22:1*

Boaz said to Ruth:
"All my fellow townsmen know that you are a woman of
noble character."

—*Ruth 3:11*

Don't let anyone look down on you because you are
young, but set an example for the believers in speech,
in life, in love, in faith and in purity.

—*1 Timothy 4:12*

Week 43: Monday

When a mocker is punished, the simple gain wisdom;
when a wise man is instructed, he gets
knowledge.

—Proverbs 21:11

Turn from evil and do good;
then you will dwell in the land forever.
For the LORD loves the just
and will not forsake his faithful ones.

They will be protected forever,
but the offspring of the wicked will be cut off;
the righteous will inherit the land
and dwell in it forever.

—Psalm 37:27–29

Week 43: Tuesday

Flog a mocker, and the simple will learn prudence;
    rebuke a discerning man, and he will gain
    knowledge.

—Proverbs 19:25

"You disciplined me like an unruly calf,
    and I have been disciplined.
Restore me, and I will return,
    because you are the LORD my God.
After I strayed,
    I repented;
after I came to understand."

—Jeremiah 31:18–19

Those who sow in tears
    will reap with songs of joy.
He who goes out weeping,
    carrying seed to sow,
will return with songs of joy,
    carrying sheaves with him.

—Psalm 126:5–6

Week 43: Wednesday

Blessed is he
>   whose transgressions are forgiven,
>   whose sins are covered.
Blessed is the man
>   whose sin the LORD does not count against him
>   and in whose spirit is no deceit.

When I kept silent,
>   my bones wasted away
>   through my groaning all day long.
For day and night
>   your hand was heavy upon me;
my strength was sapped
>   as in the heat of summer.

Then I acknowledged my sin to you
>   and did not cover up my iniquity.
I said, "I will confess
>   my transgressions to the LORD"—
and you forgave
>   the guilt of my sin.

—*Psalm 32:1–5*

Week 43: Thursday

Moses took his seat to serve as judge for the people, and they stood around him from morning till evening. When his father-in-law saw all that Moses was doing for the people, he said, . . . "What you are doing is not good. You and these people who come to you will only wear yourselves out. The work is too heavy for you; you cannot handle it alone. Listen now to me and I will give you some advice, and may God be with you. You must be the people's representative before God and bring their disputes to him. Teach them the decrees and laws, and show them the way to live and the duties they are to perform. But select capable men from all the people . . . and appoint them as officials over thousands, hundreds, fifties and tens. Have them serve as judges for the people at all times, but have them bring every difficult case to you; the simple cases they can decide themselves. That will make your load lighter, because they will share it with you. If you do this and God so commands, you will be able to stand the strain, . . ." Moses listened to his father-in-law and did everything he said. He chose capable men from all Israel and made them leaders of the people, officials over thousands, hundreds, fifties and tens. They served as judges for the people at all times. The difficult cases they brought to Moses, but the simple ones they decided themselves.

—Exodus 18:13–14, 17–26

Week 43: Friday

Whoever loves discipline loves knowledge,
but he who hates correction is stupid.

—Proverbs 12:1

My brothers, if one of you should wander from the truth and someone should bring him back, remember this: Whoever turns a sinner from the error of his way will save him from death and cover over a multitude of sins.

—James 5:19–20

He who conceals his sins does not prosper,
but whoever confesses and renounces them
finds mercy.

—Proverbs 28:13

Week 43: Weekend

Remember, O LORD, your great mercy and love,
*   for they are from of old.*
Remember not the sins of my youth
*   and my rebellious ways;*
according to your love remember me,
*   for you are good, O LORD.*

Good and upright is the LORD;
*   therefore he instructs sinners in his ways.*
He guides the humble in what is right
*   and teaches them his way.*
All the ways of the LORD are loving and faithful
*   for those who keep the demands of his covenant.*
For the sake of your name, O LORD,
*   forgive my iniquity, though it is great.*
Who, then, is the man that fears the LORD?
*   He will instruct him in the way chosen for him.*
He will spend his days in prosperity,
*   and his descendants will inherit the land.*
The LORD confides in those who fear him;
*   he makes his covenant known to them.*
My eyes are ever on the LORD,
*   for only he will release my feet from the snare.*

—Psalm 25:6–15

Week 44: Monday

*Does the Lord delight in burnt offerings and sacrifices
    as much as in obeying the voice of the Lord?
To obey is better than sacrifice,
    and to heed is better than the fat of rams.*

—1 Samuel 15:22

Submit to one another out of reverence for Christ.

—Ephesians 5:21

*Is not wisdom found among the aged?
    Does not long life bring understanding?*

—Job 12:12

Week 44: Tuesday

There a centurion's servant, whom his master valued highly, was sick and about to die. The centurion heard of Jesus and sent some elders of the Jews to him, asking him to come and heal his servant. When they came to Jesus, they pleaded earnestly with him, "This man deserves to have you do this, because he loves our nation and has built our synagogue." So Jesus went with them.

He was not far from the house when the centurion sent friends to say to him: "Lord, don't trouble yourself, for I do not deserve to have you come under my roof. That is why I did not even consider myself worthy to come to you. But say the word, and my servant will be healed. For I myself am a man under authority, with soldiers under me. I tell this one, 'Go,' and he goes; and that one, 'Come,' and he comes. I say to my servant, 'Do this,' and he does it."

When Jesus heard this, he was amazed at him, and turning to the crowd following him, he said, "I tell you, I have not found such great faith even in Israel." Then the men who had been sent returned to the house and found the servant well.

—Luke 7:2–10

Week 44: Wednesday

Everyone must submit himself to the governing authorities, for there is no authority except that which God has established. The authorities that exist have been established by God. Consequently, he who rebels against the authority is rebelling against what God has instituted, and those who do so will bring judgment on themselves. For rulers hold no terror for those who do right, but for those who do wrong. Do you want to be free from fear of the one in authority? Then do what is right and he will commend you. For he is God's servant to do you good. But if you do wrong, be afraid, for he does not bear the sword for nothing. He is God's servant, an agent of wrath to bring punishment on the wrongdoer. Therefore, it is necessary to submit to the authorities, not only because of possible punishment but also because of conscience. This is also why you pay taxes, for the authorities are God's servants, who give their full time to governing. Give everyone what you owe him: If you owe taxes, pay taxes; if revenue, then revenue; if respect, then respect; if honor, then honor.

—Romans 13:1–7

Week 44: Thursday

Now we ask you, brothers, to respect those who work hard among you, who are over you in the Lord and who admonish you. Hold them in the highest regard in love because of their work.

—1 Thessalonians 5:12–13

Obey your leaders and submit to their authority. They keep watch over you as men who must give an account. Obey them so that their work will be a joy, not a burden, for that would be of no advantage to you.

—Hebrews 13:17

Slaves, submit yourselves to your masters with all respect, not only to those who are good and considerate, but also to those who are harsh.

—1 Peter 2:18

Week 44: Friday

Remind the people to be subject to rulers and authorities, to be obedient, to be ready to do whatever is good, to slander no one, to be peaceable and considerate, and to show true humility toward all men.

—Titus 3:1–2

I urge that requests, prayers, intercession and thanksgiving be made for everyone—for kings and all those in authority, that we may live peaceful and quiet lives in all godliness and holiness. This is good, and pleases God our Savior.

—1 Timothy 2:1–3

Week 44: Weekend

Submit yourselves for the Lord's sake to every authority instituted among men: whether to the king, as the supreme authority, or to governors, who are sent by him to punish those who do wrong and to commend those who do right.
For it is God's will that by doing good you should silence the ignorant talk of foolish men. Live as free men, but do not use your freedom as a cover-up for evil; live as servants of God. Show proper respect to everyone: Love the brotherhood of believers, fear God, honor the king.

—1 Peter 2:13–17

Remember your leaders, who spoke the word of God to you. Consider the outcome of their way of life and imitate their faith.

—Hebrews 13:7

Week 45: Monday

If sinners entice you,
do not give in to them.
If they say, "Come along with us;
let's lie in wait for someone's blood,
let's waylay some harmless soul;
let's swallow them alive, like the grave,
and whole, like those who go down to the pit;
we will get all sorts of valuable things
and fill our houses with plunder;
throw in your lot with us,
and we will share a common purse"—
do not go along with them,
do not set foot on their paths;
for their feet rush into sin,
they are swift to shed blood.
How useless to spread a net
in full view of all the birds!
These men lie in wait for their own blood;
they waylay only themselves!
Such is the end of all who go after ill-gotten gain;
it takes away the lives of those who get it.

—Proverbs 1:10–19

Week 45: Tuesday

Submit yourselves ... to God. Resist the devil, and he will flee from you. Come near to God and he will come near to you.

—James 4:7–8

Jesus shared in our humanity so that by his death he might destroy him who holds the power of death—that is, the devil— and free those who all their lives were held in slavery by their fear of death.

—Hebrews 2:14–15

Since we have a great high priest who has gone through the heavens, Jesus the Son of God, let us hold firmly to the faith we profess. For we do not have a high priest who is unable to sympathize with our weaknesses, but we have one who has been tempted in every way, just as we are—yet was without sin. Let us then approach the throne of grace with confidence, so that we may receive mercy and find grace to help us in our time of need.

—Hebrews 4:14–16

Week 45: Wednesday

When tempted, no one should say, "God is tempting me." For God cannot be tempted by evil, nor does he tempt anyone; but each one is tempted when, by his own evil desire, he is dragged away and enticed.

—James 1:13–14

Do not give the devil a foothold. He who has been stealing must steal no longer, but must work, doing something useful with his own hands, that he may have something to share with those in need.

—Ephesians 4:27–28

People who want to get rich fall into temptation and a trap and into many foolish and harmful desires that plunge men into ruin and destruction. For the love of money is a root of all kinds of evil. Some people, eager for money, have wandered from the faith and pierced themselves with many griefs.

—1 Timothy 6:9–10

Week 45: Thursday

If we walk in the light, as he is in the light, we have fellowship with one another, and the blood of Jesus, his Son, purifies us from all sin.
If we claim to be without sin, we deceive ourselves and the truth is not in us. If we confess our sins, he is faithful andjust and will forgive us our sins and purify us from all unrighteousness.

—1 John 1:7–9

Your enemy the devil prowls around like a roaring lion looking for someone to devour. Resist him, standing firm in the faith, because you know that your brothers throughout the world are undergoing the same kind of sufferings.

—1 Peter 5:8–9

Watch and pray so that you will not fall into temptation. The spirit is willing, but the body is weak.

—Mark 14:38

Week 45: Friday

Dear friend, do not imitate what is evil but what is good. Anyone who does what is good is from God. Anyone who does what is evil has not seen God.

—3 John 11

Lead us not into temptation,
    but deliver us from the evil one.

—Matthew 6:13

No temptation has seized you except what is common to man. And God is faithful; he will not let you be tempted beyond what you can bear. But when you are tempted, he will also provide a way out so that you can stand up under it.

—1 Corinthians 10:13

Who can discern his errors?
    Forgive my hidden faults.
Keep your servant also from willful sins;
    may they not rule over me.
Then will I be blameless,
    innocent of great transgression.

—Psalm 19:12–13

Week 45: Weekend

Jesus was led by the Spirit into the desert to be tempted by the devil. After fasting forty days and forty nights,
he was hungry. The tempter came to him and said, "If
you are the Son of God, tell these stones to become
bread."

Jesus answered, "It is written: 'Man does not live on
bread alone, but on every word that comes from the
mouth of God.' "

Then the devil took him to the holy city and had him
stand on the highest point of the temple. "If you are the
Son of God," he said, "throw yourself down. For it is
written:

" 'He will command his angels concerning you,
    and they will lift you up in their hands,
so that you will not strike your foot against a stone.' "

Jesus answered him, "It is also written: 'Do not put the
Lord your God to the test.'"

Again, the devil took him to a very high mountain and
showed him all the kingdoms of the world and their
splendor. "All this I will give you," he said, "if you will
bow down and worship me."

Jesus said to him, "Away from me, Satan! For it is written: 'Worship the Lord your God, and serve him only.' "
Then the devil left him.

—*Matthew 4:1–11*

Week 46: Monday

Do not be yoked together with unbelievers. For what do righteousness and wickedness have in common? Or what fellowship can light have with darkness? What harmony is there between Christ and Belial? What does a believer have in common with an unbeliever? What agreement is there between the temple of God and idols? For we are the temple of the living God. As God has said: "I will live with them and walk among them, and I will be their God, and they will be my people."

"Therefore come out from them
and be separate,
says the Lord.
Touch no unclean thing,
and I will receive you."
"I will be a Father to you,
and you will be my sons and daughters,
says the Lord Almighty."

—2 Corinthians 6:14–18

Week 46: Tuesday

Have mercy on me, O God, have mercy on me,
  for in you my soul takes refuge.
I will take refuge in the shadow of your wings
  until the disaster has passed.

I cry out to God Most High,
  to God, who fulfills his purpose for me.
He sends from heaven and saves me,
  rebuking those who hotly pursue me;
  God sends his love and his faithfulness.

I am in the midst of lions;
  I lie among ravenous beasts—
men whose teeth are spears and arrows,
  whose tongues are sharp swords. . . .

They spread a net for my feet—
  I was bowed down in distress.
They dug a pit in my path—
  but they have fallen into it themselves.

My heart is steadfast, O God,
  my heart is steadfast.

—Psalm 57:1–4, 6–7

Week 46: Wednesday

Dear friends, I urge you, as aliens and strangers in the
world, to abstain from sinful desires, which war against
your soul. Live such good lives among the pagans that,
though they accuse you of doing wrong, they may see
your good deeds and glorify God on the day he visits us.

—1 Peter 2:11–12

A little while, and the wicked will be no more;
   though you look for them, they will not be found.
But the meek will inherit the land
   and enjoy great peace.

The wicked plot against the righteous
   and gnash their teeth at them;
but the Lord laughs at the wicked,
   for he knows their day is coming.

Better the little that the righteous have
   than the wealth of many wicked;
for the power of the wicked will be broken,
   but the LORD upholds the righteous.

—Psalm 37:10–13, 16-

17

Week 46: Thursday

Be very strong; be careful to obey all that is written in
the Book of the Law of Moses, without turning aside to
the right or to the left. Do not associate with these
nations that remain among you; do not invoke the
names of their gods or swear by them. You must not
serve them or bow down to them. But you are to hold
fast to the LORD your God, as you have until now.

—Joshua 23:6–8

The Israelites said to Samuel:
"Appoint a king to lead us, such as all the other nations
have."
But when they said, "Give us a king to lead us," this
displeased Samuel; so he prayed to the LORD. And the
LORD told him: ". . . It is not you they have rejected, but
they have rejected me as their king."
But the people refused to listen to Samuel. "No!" they
said. "We want a king over us. then we will be like all
the other nations, with a king to lead us and to go out
before us and fight our battles."

—1 Samuel 8:5–7, 19–20

Week 46: Friday

Nebuchadnezzar king of Babylon came to Jerusalem . . .
the king ordered Ashpenaz, chief of his court officials,
to bring in some of the Israelites from the royal family
and the nobility—young men without any physical
defect, handsome, showing aptitude for every kind of
learning, well informed, quick to understand, and
qualified to serve in the king's palace. . . . The king
assigned them a daily amount of food and wine from the
king's table. They were to be trained for three years,
and after that they were to enter the king's service.
Among these were some from Judah: Daniel, Hananiah,
Mishael and Azariah. . . . But Daniel . . . asked the chief
official for permission not to defile himself this way. . . .
but the official told Daniel, "I am afraid of my lord the
king, who has assigned your food and drink. Why should
he see you looking worse than the other young men
your age? The king would then have my head because
of you." Daniel then said to the guard whom the chief
official had appointed over Daniel, Hananiah, Mishael
and Azariah, "Please test your servants for ten days:
Give us nothing but vegetables to eat and water to
drink. Then compare our appearance with that of the
young men who eat the royal food, and treat your servants in accordance with what you see." So he agreed
to this and tested them for ten days. At the end of the
ten days they looked healthier and better nourished
than any of the young men who ate the royal food.

—Daniel 1:1, 3–6, 8, 10–15

Week 46: Weekend

Blessed is the man
  who does not walk in the counsel of the wicked
or stand in the way of sinners
  or sit in the seat of mockers.
But his delight is in the law of the LORD,
  and on his law he meditates day and night.
He is like a tree planted by streams of water,
  which yields its fruit in season
and whose leaf does not wither.
Whatever he does prospers.
Not so the wicked!
They are like chaff
  that the wind blows away.
Therefore the wicked will not stand in the judgment,
  nor sinners in the assembly of the righteous.
For the LORD watches over the way of the righteous,
  but the way of the wicked will perish.

—Psalm 1

Week 47: Monday

When they had crucified Jesus, they divided up his clothes by casting lots. And sitting down, they kept watch over him there. Above his head they placed the written charge against him: THIS IS JESUS, THE KING OF THE JEWS. Two robbers were crucified with him, one on his right and one on his left. Those who passed by hurled insults at him, shaking their heads and saying, "You who are going to destroy the temple and build it in three days, save yourself! Come down from the cross, if you are the Son of God!"

In the same way the chief priests, the teachers of the law and the elders mocked him. "He saved others," they said, "but he can't save himself! He's the King of Israel! Let him come down now from the cross, and we will believe in him. He trusts in God. Let God rescue him now if he wants him, for he said, 'I am the Son of God.' " In the same way the robbers who were crucified with him also heaped insults on him.

From the sixth hour until the ninth hour darkness came over all the land. About the ninth hour Jesus cried out in a loud voice, "Eloi, Eloi, lama sabachthani?"—which means, "My God, my God, why have you forsaken me?"

—Matthew 27:35–46

Week 47: Tuesday

Joseph's brothers plotted [against] him. . . . "Come now, let's . . . throw him into one of these cisterns and say that a ferocious animal devoured him." . . .

So when Joseph came to his brothers, . . . they took him and threw him into the cistern. . . .

When the Midianite merchants came by, his brothers pulled Joseph up out of the cistern and sold him for twenty shekels of silver to the Ishmaelites, who took him to Egypt. . . .

Pharaoh said to Joseph, "Since God has made [the meaning of my dream] known to you, there is no one so discerning and wise as you. You shall be in charge of my palace, and all my people are to submit to your orders." . . .

When Joseph's brothers [met him in Egypt years later] they said, "What if Joseph holds a grudge against us and pays us back for all the wrongs we did to him?" . . .

His brothers then came and threw themselves down before him. "We are your slaves," they said.

But Joseph said to them, "Don't be afraid. Am I in the place of God? You intended to harm me, but God intended it for good to accomplish what is now being done, the saving of many lives. So then, don't be afraid. I will provide for you and your children." And he reassured them and spoke kindly to them.

—*Genesis 37:18–20, 23–24, 28; 41:39–40; 50:15, 18–21*

Week 47: Wednesday

For men are not cast off
by the LORD forever.
Though he brings grief, he will show compassion,
so great is his unfailing love.
For he does not willingly bring affliction
or grief to the children of men.

—Lamentations 3:31–33

Out of the depths I cry to you, O LORD;
O Lord, hear my voice.
Let your ears be attentive
to my cry for mercy....
I wait for the LORD, my soul waits,
and in his word I put my hope.

—Psalm 130:1–2, 5

My God, my God, why have you forsaken me?
Why are you so far from saving me,
so far from the words of my groaning?
I am ... scorned by men and despised by the people.
All who see me mock me;
they hurl insults, shaking their heads....
Do not be far from me,
for trouble is near
and there is no one to help....
You who fear the LORD, praise him!

—Psalm 22:1, 6, 11, 23

Week 47: Thursday

[Sarah] said to Abraham, "Get rid of that slave woman and her son, for that slave woman's son will never share in the inheritance with my son Isaac."

The matter distressed Abraham greatly because it concerned his son. But God said to him, "Do not be so distressed about the boy and your maidservant. Listen to whatever Sarah tells you, because it is through Isaac that your offspring will be reckoned. I will make the son of the maidservant into a nation also, because he is your offspring."

Early the next morning Abraham took some food and a skin of water and gave them to Hagar. He set them on her shoulders and then sent her off with the boy. She went on her way and wandered in the desert of Beersheba.

When the water in the skin was gone, she put the boy under one of the bushes. Then she went off and sat down nearby, about a bowshot away, for she thought, "I cannot watch the boy die." And as she sat there nearby, she began to sob.

God heard the boy crying, and the angel of God called to Hagar from heaven and said to her, "What is the matter, Hagar? Do not be afraid; God has heard the boy crying as he lies there. Lift the boy up and take him by the hand, for I will make him into a great nation."

—*Genesis 21:10–18*

Week 47: Friday

Who has believed our message
    and to whom has the arm of the LORD been
    revealed?
He grew up before him like a tender shoot,
    and like a root out of dry ground.
He had no beauty or majesty to attract us to him,
    nothing in his appearance that we should
    desire him.
He was despised and rejected by men,
    a man of sorrows, and familiar with suffering.
Like one from whom men hide their faces
    he was despised, and we esteemed him not.

Surely he took up our infirmities
    and carried our sorrows,
yet we considered him stricken by God,
    smitten by him, and afflicted.
But he was pierced for our transgressions,
    he was crushed for our iniquities;
the punishment that brought us peace was upon him,
    and by his wounds we are healed.
We all, like sheep, have gone astray,
    each of us has turned to his own way;
and the LORD has laid on him
    the iniquity of us all.

—Isaiah 53:1–6

Week 47: Weekend

O Lord, . . .
I am ridiculed all day long;
    everyone mocks me. . . .
All my friends
    are waiting for me to slip, saying,
"Perhaps he will be deceived;
    then we will prevail over him
    and take our revenge on him."

But the Lord is with me like a mighty warrior;
    so my persecutors will stumble and not prevail.
They will fail and be thoroughly disgraced;
    their dishonor will never be forgotten.
O Lord Almighty, you who examine the righteous
    and probe the heart and mind,
let me see your vengeance upon them,
    for to you I have committed my cause.

Sing to the Lord!
    Give praise to the Lord!
He rescues the life of the needy
    from the hands of the wicked.

—Jeremiah 20:7, 10–13

Week 48: Monday

[King Solomon asked God,]
"Give me wisdom and knowledge, that I may lead this people, for who is able to govern this great people of yours?" God said to Solomon, "Since this is your heart's desire . . . wisdom and knowledge will be given you."

—2 Chronicles 1:10–12

God gave Solomon wisdom and very great insight, and a breadth of understanding as measureless as the sand on the seashore. Solomon's wisdom was greater than the wisdom of all the men of the East, and greater than all the wisdom of Egypt. . . . And his fame spread to all the surrounding nations. He spoke three thousand proverbs and his songs numbered a thousand and five. He described plant life, from the cedar of Lebanon to the hyssop that grows out of walls. He also taught about animals and birds, reptiles and fish. Men of all nations came to listen to Solomon's wisdom, sent by all the kings of the world, who had heard of his wisdom.

—1 Kings 4:29–34

Week 48: Tuesday

This is the confidence we have in approaching God: that if we ask anything according to his will, he hears us. And if we know that he hears us—whatever we ask—we know that we have what we asked of him.

—1 John 5:14–15

The LORD is with you when you are with him. If you seek him, he will be found by you.

—2 Chronicles 15:2

Let everyone who is godly pray to you, Lord,
*   while you may be found;*
surely when the mighty waters rise,
*   they will not reach him.*
You are my hiding place;
*   you will protect me from trouble*
*   and surround me with songs of deliverance.*

—Psalm 32:6–7

Week 48: **Wednesday**

Jesus said,
"Ask and it will be given to you; seek and you will find;
knock and the door will be opened to you. For everyone
who asks receives; he who seeks finds; and to him
who knocks, the door will be opened.
"Which of you, if his son asks for bread, will give him a
stone? Or if he asks for a fish, will give him a snake? If
you, then, though you are evil, know how to give good
gifts to your children, how much more will your Father
in heaven give good gifts to those who ask him!"

—*Matthew 7:7–11*

The heart of the discerning acquires knowledge;
the ears of the wise seek it out.

—*Proverbs 18:15*

"You will seek me and find me when you seek me with
all your heart. I will be found by you," declares the
LORD.

—*Jeremiah 29:13–14*

Week 48: Thursday

I desire to do your will, O my God;
your law is within my heart." . . .
Do not withhold your mercy from me, O Lord;
may your love and your truth always protect me.
For troubles without number surround me;
my sins have overtaken me, and I cannot see.
They are more than the hairs of my head,
and my heart fails within me.

Be pleased, O Lord, to save me;
O Lord, come quickly to help me.
May all who seek to take my life
be put to shame and confusion;
may all who desire my ruin
be turned back in disgrace.
May those who say to me, "Aha! Aha!"
be appalled at their own shame.
But may all who seek you
rejoice and be glad in you;
may those who love your salvation always say,
"The Lord be exalted!"

Yet I am poor and needy;
may the Lord think of me.
You are my help and my deliverer;
O my God, do not delay.

—Psalm 40:8, 11–17

Week 48: Friday

I am always with you;
*   you hold me by my right hand, Lord.*
You guide me with your counsel,
*   and afterward you will take me into glory.*
Whom have I in heaven but you?
*   And earth has nothing I desire besides you.*

—Psalm 73:23–25

He who trusts in himself is a fool,
*   but he who walks in wisdom is kept safe.*

—Proverbs 28:26

Blessed are those who hunger and thirst for
righteousness,
*   for they will be filled.*

—Matthew 5:6

Week 48: Weekend

For he will command his angels concerning you
to guard you in all your ways.

—Psalm 91:11

The salvation of the righteous comes from the LORD.
he is their stronghold in time of trouble.
The LORD helps them and delivers them;
he delivers them from the wicked and saves them,
because they take refuge in him.

—Psalm 37:39

Daniel prayed:
"I thank and praise you, O God of my fathers:
You have given me wisdom and power,
you have made known to me what we asked of you,
you have made known to us the dream of the king."

—Daniel 2:23

Hear, O LORD, and answer me,
for I am poor and needy.
Guard my life, for I am devoted to you.
You are my God; save your servant
who trusts in you.
Have mercy on me, O Lord,
for I call to you all day long.

—Psalm 86:1–3

Week 49: Monday

Search me, O God, and know my heart;
*   test me and know my anxious thoughts.*
See if there is any offensive way in me,
*   and lead me in the way everlasting.*

—**Psalm 139:23–24**

Those who hope in the LORD
*   will renew their strength.*
They will soar on wings like eagles;
*   they will run and not grow weary,*
*   they will walk and not be faint.*

—**Isaiah 40:31**

Cast all your anxiety on God because he cares for you.

—**1 Peter 5:7**

Blessed are those who mourn,
*   for they will be comforted.*

—**Matthew 5:4**

Week 49: Tuesday

Banish anxiety from your heart
and cast off the troubles of your body.

—Ecclesiastes 11:10

"Peace, peace, to those far and near,"
says the LORD. "And I will heal them."

—Isaiah 57:19

Do not be anxious about anything, but in everything, by
prayer and petition, with thanksgiving, present your
requests to God. And the peace of God, which tran-
scends all understanding, will guard your hearts and
your minds in Christ Jesus.

—Philippians 4:6–7

Week 49: **Wednesday**

Jesus said,
"In this world you will have trouble. But take heart! I have overcome the world."

—*John 16:33*

The one who is in you is greater than the one who is in the world.

—*1 John 4:4*

*The LORD is my light and my salvation—
    whom shall I fear?
The LORD is the stronghold of my life—
    of whom shall I be afraid?
When evil men advance against me
    to devour my flesh,
when my enemies and my foes attack me,
    they will stumble and fall.
Though an army besiege me,
    my heart will not fear;
though war break out against me,
    even then will I be confident.*

—*Psalm 27:1–3*

Week 49: Thursday

When you pass through the waters,
*   I will be with you;*
and when you pass through the rivers,
*   they will not sweep over you.*
When you walk through the fire,
*   you will not be burned;*
*   the flames will not set you ablaze.*
For I am the LORD, your God,
*   the Holy One of Israel, your Savior.*

—Isaiah 43:2–3

The salvation of the righteous comes from the LORD;
*   he is their stronghold in time of trouble.*
The LORD helps them and delivers them;
*   he delivers them from the wicked and saves them,*
*   because they take refuge in him.*

—Psalm 37:39–40

Week 49: Friday

Jesus said,
"I tell you, do not worry about your life, what you will eat or drink; or about your body, what you will wear. Is not life more important than food, and the body more important than clothes? Look at the birds of the air; they do not sow or reap or store away in barns, and yet your heavenly Father feeds them. Are you not much more valuable than they? Who of you by worrying can add a single hour to his life?

"And why do you worry about clothes? See how the lilies of the field grow. They do not labor or spin. Yet I tell you that not even Solomon in all his splendor was dressed like one of these. If that is how God clothes the grass of the field, which is here today and tomorrow is thrown into the fire, will he not much more clothe you, O you of little faith? So do not worry, saying, 'What shall we eat?' or 'What shall we drink?' or 'What shall we wear?' For the pagans run after all these things, and your heavenly Father knows that you need them. But seek first his kingdom and his righteousness, and all these things will be given to you as well. Therefore do not worry about tomorrow, for tomorrow will worry about itself. Each day has enough trouble of its own."

—Matthew 6:25–34

Week 49: Weekend

We know that in all things God works for the good of those who love him, who have been called according to his purpose. . . . If God is for us, who can be against us? He who did not spare his own Son, but gave him up for us all—how will he not also, along with him, graciously give us all things? . . . Who shall separate us from the love of Christ? Shall trouble or hardship or persecution or famine or nakedness or danger or sword? . . . No, in all these things we are more than conquerors through him who loved us. For I am convinced that neither death nor life, neither angels nor demons, neither the present nor the future, nor any powers, neither height nor depth, nor anything else in all creation, will be able to separate us from the love of God that is in Christ Jesus our Lord.

—Romans 8:28, 31–32, 35, 37–39

Who will rise up for me against the wicked?
    Who will take a stand for me against evildoers?
Unless the LORD had given me help,
    I would soon have dwelt in the silence of death.
When I said, "My foot is slipping,"
    your love, O LORD, supported me.
When anxiety was great within me,
    your consolation brought joy to my soul.

—Psalm 94:16–19

Week 50: Monday

I waited patiently for the LORD;
*   he turned to me and heard my cry.*
He lifted me out of the slimy pit,
*   out of the mud and mire;*
he set my feet on a rock
*   and gave me a firm place to stand.*
He put a new song in my mouth,
*   a hymn of praise to our God.*
Many will see and fear
*   and put their trust in the LORD.*

Blessed is the man
*   who makes the LORD his trust,*
who does not look to the proud,
*   to those who turn aside to false gods.*
Many, O LORD my God,
*   are the wonders you have done.*
The things you planned for us
*   no one can recount to you;*
were I to speak and tell of them,
*   they would be too many to declare.*

—Psalm 40:1–5

Week 50: Tuesday

But you, O Sovereign LORD,
  deal well with me for your name's sake;
  out of the goodness of your love, deliver me.
For I am poor and needy,
  and my heart is wounded within me.
I fade away like an evening shadow;
  I am shaken off like a locust.
My knees give way from fasting;
  my body is thin and gaunt.
I am an object of scorn to my accusers;
  when they see me, they shake their heads.

Help me, O LORD my God;
  save me in accordance with your love.

—Psalm 109:21–26

Week 50: Wednesday

I love you, O LORD, my strength.

The LORD is my rock, my fortress and my deliverer;
my God is my rock, in whom I take refuge.
He is my shield and the horn of my salvation,
my stronghold.
I call to the LORD, who is worthy of praise,
and I am saved from my enemies.

The cords of death entangled me;
the torrents of destruction overwhelmed me.
The cords of the grave coiled around me;
the snares of death confronted me.
In my distress I called to the LORD;
I cried to my God for help.
From his temple he heard my voice;
my cry came before him, into his ears. . . .
He reached down from on high and took hold of me;
he drew me out of deep waters.
He rescued me from my powerful enemy,
from my foes, who were too strong for me.
They confronted me in the day of my disaster,
but the LORD was my support.
He brought me out into a spacious place;
he rescued me because he delighted in me.

—Psalm 18:1–6, 16–19

Week 50: Thursday

I lift up my eyes to the hills—
*   where does my help come from?*
My help comes from the Lord,
*   the Maker of heaven and earth.*

He will not let your foot slip—
*   he who watches over you will not slumber;*
indeed, he who watches over Israel
*   will neither slumber nor sleep.*

The Lord watches over you—
*   the Lord is your shade at your right hand;*
the sun will not harm you by day,
*   nor the moon by night.*

The Lord will keep you from all harm—
*   he will watch over your life;*
the Lord will watch over your coming and going
*   both now and forevermore.*

—Psalm 121:1–8

Week 50: Friday

Sing to God, O kingdoms of the earth,
    sing praise to the Lord,
to him who rides the ancient skies above,
    who thunders with mighty voice.
Proclaim the power of God,
    whose majesty is over Israel,
    whose power is in the skies.
You are awesome, O God, in your sanctuary;
    the God of Israel gives power and strength
    to his people.

—Psalm 68:32–35

As for God, his way is perfect;
    the word of the LORD is flawless.
He is a shield
    for all who take refuge in him.
For who is God besides the LORD?
    And who is the Rock except our God?
It is God who arms me with strength
    and makes my way perfect.
He makes my feet like the feet of a deer;
    he enables me to stand on the heights.

—2 Samuel 22:31–34

Week 50: Weekend

Hear my voice when I call, O LORD;
*   be merciful to me and answer me.*
My heart says of you, "Seek his face!"
*   Your face, LORD, I will seek.*
Do not hide your face from me,
*   do not turn your servant away in anger;*
*   you have been my helper.*
Do not reject me or forsake me,
*   O God my Savior.*

Though my father and mother forsake me,
*   the LORD will receive me.*
Teach me your way, O LORD;
*   lead me in a straight path*
*   because of my oppressors.*

—Psalm 27:7-11

Very early in the morning, while it was still dark, Jesus got up, left the house and went off to a solitary place, where he prayed.

—Mark 1:35

The LORD is good,
*   a refuge in times of trouble.*
He cares for those who trust in him.

—Nahum 1:7

Week 51: Monday

*The LORD has dealt with me according to my
righteousness;*
    *according to the cleanness of my hands he has
    rewarded me.*
For I have kept the ways of the LORD;
    I have not done evil by turning from my God.
All his laws are before me;
    I have not turned away from his decrees.
I have been blameless before him
    and have kept myself from sin.
*The LORD has rewarded me according to my
righteousness,*
    *according to the cleanness of my hands in
    his sight.*

To the faithful you show yourself faithful,
    to the blameless you show yourself blameless,
to the pure you show yourself pure,
    but to the crooked you show yourself shrewd.

—Psalm 18:20–26

Week 51: Tuesday

He who works his land will have abundant food,
but the one who chases fantasies will have his fill
of poverty.

—Proverbs 28:19

The sins of some men are obvious, reaching the place
of judgment ahead of them; the sins of others trail
behind them. In the same way, good deeds are obvious, and even those that are not cannot be hidden.

—1 Timothy 5:24–25

What the wicked dreads will overtake him;
what the righteous desire will be granted.

—Proverbs 10:24

The wages of the righteous bring them life,
but the income of the wicked brings them
punishment.

—Proverbs 10:16

Week 51: **Wednesday**

Remember this: Whoever sows sparingly will also reap sparingly, and whoever sows generously will also reap generously. Each man should give what he has decided in his heart to give, not reluctantly or under compulsion, for God loves a cheerful giver. And God is able to make all grace abound to you, so that in all things at all times, having all that you need, you will abound in every good work. As it is written:

"He has scattered abroad his gifts to the poor;
his righteousness endures forever."

Now he who supplies seed to the sower and bread for food will also supply and increase your store of seed and will enlarge the harvest of your righteousness. You will be made rich in every way so that you can be generous on every occasion, and through us your generosity will result in thanksgiving to God.

This service that you perform is not only supplying the needs of God's people but is also overflowing in many expressions of thanks to God. Because of the service by which you have proved yourselves, men will praise God for the obedience that accompanies your confession of the gospel of Christ, and for your generosity in sharing with them and with everyone else. And in their prayers for you their hearts will go out to you, because of the surpassing grace God has given you. Thanks be to God for his indescribable gift!

—2 Corinthians 9:6–15

Week 51: Thursday

God is not unjust; he will not forget your work and the love you have shown him as you have helped his people and continue to help them.

—*Hebrews 6:10*

Jesus said,
"Behold, I am coming soon! My reward is with me, and I will give to everyone according to what he has done. I am the Alpha and the Omega, the First and the Last, the Beginning and the End."

—*Revelation 22:12–13*

Those who sow in tears
   will reap with songs of joy.

—*Psalm 126:5*

Week 51: Friday

"Make a tree good and its fruit will be good, or make a tree bad and its fruit will be bad, for a tree is recognized by its fruit. ... For out of the overflow of the heart the mouth speaks. The good man brings good things out of the good stored up in him, and the evil man brings evil things out of the evil stored up in him. By your words you will be acquitted, and by your words you will be condemned."

—Matthew 12:33–35, 37

Sow for yourselves righteousness,
  reap the fruit of unfailing love,
and break up your unplowed ground;
  for it is time to seek the LORD,
    until he comes
    and showers righteousness on you.

—Hosea 10:12

Week 51: Weekend

Do not be deceived: God cannot be mocked. A man reaps what he sows. The one who sows to please his sinful nature, from that nature will reap destruction; the one who sows to please the Spirit will reap eternal life.

—*Galatians 6:7–8*

Anyone who does wrong will be repaid for his wrong, and there is no favoritism.

—*Colossians 3:25*

One thing God has spoken,
  two things have I heard:
that you, O God, are strong,
  and that you, O Lord, are loving.
Surely you will reward each person
  according to what he has done.

—*Psalm 62:11–12*

Week 52: **Monday**

The fear of the LORD is the beginning of wisdom;
all who follow his precepts have good
understanding.
To him belongs eternal praise.

—Psalm 111:10

If any of you lacks wisdom, he should ask God, who
gives generously to all without finding fault, and it will
be given to him.

—James 1:5

Blessed is the man who finds wisdom,
the man who gains understanding,
for she is more profitable than silver
and yields better returns than gold. . . .
She is a tree of life to those who embrace her;
those who lay hold of her will be blessed.

—Proverbs 3:13–14, 18

Week 52: Tuesday

Who is wise and understanding among you? Let him show it by his good life, by deeds done in the humility that comes from wisdom. The wisdom that comes from heaven is first of all pure; then peace-loving, considerate, submissive, full of mercy and good fruit, impartial and sincere.

—James 3:13, 17

Wise men store up knowledge,
but the mouth of a fool invites ruin.

—Proverbs 10:14

Wisdom is supreme; therefore get wisdom.
Though it cost all you have, get understanding.

—Proverbs 4:7

Week 52: Wednesday

Where can wisdom be found?
 Where does understanding dwell?
Man does not comprehend its worth;
 it cannot be found in the land of the living.
The deep says, 'It is not in me';
 the sea says, 'It is not with me.'
It cannot be bought with the finest gold,
 nor can its price be weighed in silver.
It cannot be bought with the gold of Ophir,
 with precious onyx or sapphires.
Neither gold nor crystal can compare with it,
 nor can it be had for jewels of gold.
Coral and jasper are not worthy of mention;
 the price of wisdom is beyond rubies.
The topaz of Cush cannot compare with it;
 it cannot be bought with pure gold.

—Job 28:12–19

Week 52: Thursday

Wisdom, like an inheritance, is a good thing
    and benefits those who see the sun.
Wisdom is a shelter
    as money is a shelter,
but the advantage of knowledge is this:
    that wisdom preserves the life of its possessor.

—Ecclesiastes 7:11–12

Who is like the wise man?
    Who knows the explanation of things?
Wisdom brightens a man's face
    and changes its hard appearance.

—Ecclesiastes 8:1

The wisdom of the prudent is to give thought to their ways,
    but the folly of fools is deception.

—Proverbs 14:8

Week 52: Friday

"For my thoughts are not your thoughts,
neither are your ways my ways,"
declares the LORD.
"As the heavens are higher than the earth,
so are my ways higher than your ways
and my thoughts than your thoughts.
As the rain and the snow
come down from heaven,
and do not return to it
without watering the earth
and making it bud and flourish,
so that it yields seed for the sower and bread for
the eater,
so is my word that goes out from my mouth:
It will not return to me empty,
but will accomplish what I desire
and achieve the purpose for which I sent it."

—Isaiah 55:8–11

Week 52: Weekend

There was once a small city with only a few people in it. And a powerful king came against it, surrounded it and built huge siegeworks against it. Now there lived in that city a man poor but wise, and he saved the city by his wisdom.

—Ecclesiastes 9:14–15

Oh, the depth of the riches of the wisdom and knowledge of God!
> *How unsearchable his judgments,*
> *and his paths beyond tracing out!*
"Who has known the mind of the Lord?
> *Or who has been his counselor?"*
"Who has ever given to God,
> *that God should repay him?"*
For from him and through him and to him are all things.
> *To him be the glory forever! Amen.*

—Romans 11:33–36

At Inspirio, we love to hear from you—your
stories, your feedback,
and your product ideas.
Please send your comments to us
by way of email at
icares@zondervan.com
or to the address below:

Ψ

inspirio

Attn: Inspirio Cares
5300 Patterson Avenue SE
Grand Rapids, MI 49530

If you would like further information
about Inspirio and the products we
create, please visit us at:
www.inspiriogifts.com

Thank you and God bless!